D0271746

SCONE WITH
THE WIND

SCONE WITH THE WIND

Cakes & Bakes with a Literary Twist

Miss Victoria Sponge

CONTENTS

CONTENTS

'I declare after all there is no enjoyment
like reading! How much sooner one tires
of anything than of a book!'

Jane Austen, *Pride and Prejudice*

INTRODUCTION

NOTHING IS MORE ENJOYABLE THAN CURLING UP WITH A GOOD BOOK, UNTIL NOW THAT IS. WITH *SCONE WITH THE WIND*, YOU CAN TUCK INTO A GOOD BOOK *AND* A PIECE OF CAKE. A VERY ENJOYABLE PROSPECT INDEED.

There is something strikingly special about each and every cake and bake in this book. For these are not just any recipes, these are recipes with a literary twist. The Jane Éclair, the Key Lime & Punishment, Wuthering Bites and the Mansfield Tart. Within these pages your favourite bakes find a connection with your best-loved books to produce a mouthwatering masterpiece that always ends happily ever after. It's a novel way to get into the classics that is both bite-sized and easily digestible.

So here you can magic up the Midsummer Pudding's Dream or experiment with the Strange Cake of Dr Jelly & Mr H'Ice Cream. Bake for your big brother the Nineteen-Eighty Petits Fours, or get the gang together for a slice of Brighton Rock 'n' Roll. From thrillers to romances, children's books to plays, coming-of-age tales to dystopian dramas, every genre cooks up a storm in this tasty *tour de force*.

As well as 72 delicious recipes, each with an idiosyncratic introduction to whisk you from the kitchen to the literary world, we've also included some menu ideas to help you create themed afternoon teas, parties, picnics and book club meetings.

Prepare to discover some culinary creations that are just as imaginative as the classic stories we know and love. A coconut pavlova to carry you away to the Caribbean romance of *Love in the Time of Cholera*; an icy cool grapefruit-and-gin sorbet to summon up the bootlegged bluster of *The Great Gatsby*, and the perfect blend of chocolate and childhood nostalgia in our Charlie & the Chocolate Brownies to transport you to Willy Wonka's factory.

Are you sitting comfortably?
Then we'll begin...

THERE REALLY IS SOMETHING FOR
EVERYONE IN THIS BOOK – WHETHER
YOU'RE LOOKING FOR A KNOCKOUT
BIRTHDAY CAKE, A FANCY TART OR A
SIMPLE CRUMBLE CAKE AS THE PER-
FECT FINISH TO A SUNDAY LUNCH.
SO HAVE A GO – AND HAVE FUN!

USEFUL EQUIPMENT
Here's a list of equipment you will find
very useful when making the cakes,
bakes and goodies in this book:

› large mixing bowl
› small bowls – for icings and fillings
› measuring jug
› set of digital scales
› set of measuring spoons – ranging
  from teaspoon to tablespoon
› set of round cookie cutters
› wooden spoons, teaspoons,
  dessertspoon and a large metal spoon
› hand whisk and an electric hand whisk
  (makes beating so much quicker)

› sharp knife, a round-ended knife and a
  small serrated knife
› rolling pin
› palette knife – perfect for spreading
  icing on top of cakes and lifting
  biscuits and bakes from trays
› flexible plastic spatula – ideal for
  scraping cake mixture out of bowls
  into tins
› small and medium-sized saucepans
› couple of baking sheets
› lots of non-stick baking paper and
  paper cupcake and muffin cases.
› cling film, foil and baking beans – for
  blind baking
› kitchen sugar thermometer (very
  important to achieve the correct
  temperature when deep-frying and
  making marshmallows)
› piping bag and nozzles – 0.5cm round,
  1cm round and star-shaped, and 1.5cm
  round and star-shaped nozzles are
  used in this book.
› a selection of cake tins – square and
  round; 20cm/8in round, 20 x 20cm/

BAKING
ESSENTIALS

8 x 8in square, 20 x 30cm/8 x 12in rectangle, 23cm/9in loose-bottomed tart tin, 12-hole muffin tin
› a selection of small ovenproof ramekins
› oven gloves and dry tea towels

BASIC INGREDIENTS & COOK'S NOTES

The great thing about these recipes is that they all use accessible, easy-to-find ingredients. But here are a few tips and notes anyway to make sure that your baking is as easy as can be - and gives delicious results.

BUTTER - always use unsalted unless otherwise stated.

EGGS - should be large unless otherwise specified. These are best used at room temperature, and whenever possible should be free range. Uncooked or partially cooked eggs should not be eaten by the very young, very old, pregnant or immunocompromised people.

FOOD COLOURING - for the best results, use food colouring paste, which is available in cook shops or good supermarkets. If you prefer to use a natural food colouring, use it cautiously as some brands can affect the resulting bake and can impart a taste in the finished bake and/or topping.

SERVING SIZE - the number of cakes or serving size specified in these recipes should be viewed as a guide.

COOKING - get to know your oven, identify any hot spots and cold spots. If you're not sure, you can buy an inexpensive oven thermometer to check your oven is running at the correct temperature. Never open the oven door in the first 20 minutes of baking a cake, as your cake may sink in the middle.

EATING AND STORAGE - this is the best bit! Most cakes and bakes are best eaten on the day they are made (unless otherwise stated). If you are using a fresh cream, soft cheese, or custard filling/topping, make sure your bake is kept chilled until ready to serve. If you have leftovers, store them in an airtight container and refrigerate as necessary.

'It is narrow-minded in (men) to say that (women) ought to confine themselves to making puddings.'

—

Charlotte Brontë, *Jane Eyre*

ROMANCE & COMEDY

SCONE WITH THE WIND

CLASSIC SCONE WITH SCARLETT O'HARA STRAWBERRY JAM

~~~~~

T his delicious recipe has all the dramatic ingredients of a much-loved classic, not to mention heaps of drawling (or should we say drooling) Southern charm. It's the belle of the baked goods. What better way to enjoy these unpretentious puffs of perfection than smothered in jewelled Scarlett strawberry jam and rich, rich clouds of clotted cream? (No need to answer; it's a Rhett-orical question).

As for the age-old question as to which to layer first - the cream or the jam - frankly, my dear, I don't give a damn.

Makes 10 scones & 1 jar of jam

300g/11oz self-raising flour, plus extra for dusting
75g/2½oz butter, diced
75g/2½oz caster sugar
225–250ml/8–9fl oz milk
1 large egg, lightly beaten

>

1. To make the jam, first put a saucer in the freezer. Tip the strawberries into a heavy-based pan with the sugar and vanilla pod and heat gently, stirring, until all the sugar has dissolved and the strawberries have broken down to small pieces. Stop stirring, then squeeze in the lemon juice and increase the heat.

2. Bring to the boil and bubble for 8–10 minutes, skimming off the scum as you go. At this point the jam should be almost ready. To test for setting point, spoon a little jam onto the cold saucer. Leave to stand for a minute then push your finger through the jam – if the surface wrinkles, it is ready, if not, keep cooking and repeat the wrinkly jam test at 2-minute intervals.

3. Once the jam is ready, leave to stand for 15 minutes then remove the vanilla pod. Ladle into warm sterilised jars and seal. Set aside while you make the scones.

>

SCONE WITH
THE WIND
(cont.)

For the Scarlett O'Hara jam

500g/1lb 2oz ripe strawberries, hulled and roughly chopped

500g/1lb 2oz jam sugar

1 vanilla pod, halved

juice of ½ lemon

clotted cream, to serve

4. Heat the oven to 200C/400F/gas 6. Line a couple of baking trays with baking paper.

5. In a large bowl, rub the flour and butter together until the mixture looks like fine crumbs. Add the sugar and a pinch of salt and stir to combine. Add the milk a little at a time to make a soft dough – you may not need all of it. The dough should not be sticky.

6. Tip out the dough onto a lightly floured surface, knead briefly then press or roll out to 2.5cm (1in) thickness. Use a 6–7cm (2.5in) cutter to stamp out rounds of dough, then gather up and roll out any offcuts and stamp out more circles. Transfer to the baking tray. Brush the tops with beaten egg and bake for 12–15 minutes or until risen and golden. Remove from the oven and allow to cool completely.

7. To serve, split the scones in half and spread one half generously with jam and the other with clotted cream. Sandwich together and enjoy with a cup of tea or a glass of bubbles.

BREAKFAST AT TIFFINS

PISTACHIO AND CRANBERRY JEWELLED TIFFINS

Holly Golightly on these tempting tiffins, or you'll never fit into your Givenchy LBD. Follow the recipe and in a few quick steps - just like Holly's makeover from country girl to New York socialite - you'll have transformed the pistachios, cranberries and candied peel into an 18-carat chocolate cake.

Whether you eat these sophisticated bites for Breakfast at Tiffany's, at afternoon tea or by the light of the Moon (River), their bejewelled beauty is a decadent delight any time of day. It's true, man (Capote) - so feast on Fifth Avenue, nibble in New York and imbibe on the Upper East Side.

Makes 20 squares

250g/9oz digestive biscuits

50g/2oz pistachio nuts, roughly chopped

50g/2oz dried cranberries

50g/2oz candied peel

300g/11oz plain chocolate, roughly chopped

100g/4oz butter, diced

100g/4oz golden syrup

20 edible gems (available online or in good baking supply shops)

white baking paper and Tiffany blue ribbon, to serve (optional)

1. Line a 20 x 20cm (8 x 8in) baking tin with baking paper. Put the biscuits in a large bowl and use the end of a rolling pin to gently crush them so that you have a mixture of big chunks and small crumbs. Mix the biscuits with the nuts, cranberries and candied peel. Set aside.

2. Melt the chocolate, butter and golden syrup in a bowl set over a pan of simmering water, stirring occasionally until smooth. Pour the molten mixture over the crushed biscuit mixture and stir together until everything is combined.

3. Tip into the baking tin and flatten the top lightly. Chill for 2–3 hours or overnight. When set, cut the tiffin into 20 small squares and press an edible gem into the top of each, then wrap them in white baking paper and tie with a Tiffin-blue ribbon to serve, if you fancy. Who needs a ring anyway?

MACAROONS WITH A VIEW

WHITE CHOCOLATE AND RASPBERRY MACAROONS

~~~~~~

F lorence, Italy: a place of architectural beauty, longing, and repressed desire - especially for gelato. These ice-cream-inspired macaroons are a gentile gelato pink and crammed with an exquisite white-chocolate-and-raspberry-jam filling to echo delicious vanilla ice cream drizzled with raspberry sauce. They're sweet-as-honey(church), so don't hold back from these delicious morsels - allow your desire to run as rampant as an Edwardian society lady following her heart ...

Pack them up for a picnic in a field of violets, or find a Windy Corner to blow all your troubles away.

Makes 20 macaroons

200g/7oz icing sugar
140g/5oz ground almonds
3 egg whites
50g/2oz caster sugar
a few drops of pink food colouring

1. Sift the icing sugar and ground almonds into a bowl and whisk the two together until they are combined. Set aside.

2. In a clean bowl and using an electric whisk, beat the egg whites to soft peaks, then gradually add in the caster sugar and enough food colouring to achieve your preferred pink shade. Continue to whisk until you have stiff, shiny meringue. Gently fold the icing sugar and almond mixture into the meringues in a couple of additions until fully incorporated.

3. Line a couple of baking trays with non-stick baking paper. Spoon the mixture into a large piping bag fitted with a round 0.5cm (¼ in) nozzle, or into a large sandwich bag with the corner snipped off. Pipe forty 3cm rounds, leaving space between each one to allow for spreading. Leave to stand, uncovered, for an hour — this will help the macaroons develop a skin.

For the filling

100ml/3½fl oz double cream

1 tsp vanilla essence

100g/4oz white chocolate, roughly chopped

6 tbsp seedless raspberry jam

4. Meanwhile, make the filling. In a small pan, heat the cream and vanilla essence to just below boiling point. Remove from the heat and pour over the white chocolate in a bowl and leave to stand for 5 minutes. Stir the mixture until the chocolate has melted and the mixture is smooth, then cover and set aside until it reaches a spreadable consistency.

5. Heat the oven to 160C/325F/gas 3. Bake the macaroons for 12–15 minutes – they should be risen and have their characteristic 'legs' on show. Leave to cool on the baking paper. Sandwich together the macaroons with a small teaspoonful of raspberry jam and a smearing of white chocolate ganache.

LADY CHATTERLEY'S LAYER CAKE

TIERED FOREST FRUIT GÂTEAU

W oman cannot live by mind alone. Well, I do mind, thank you very much. Satiate your cravings and your carnal appetite with this towering layer cake, its tall, thrusting structure just rippling with overlapping woodland fruits of all varieties. Allow its fresh, fruity flavours to penetrate deep inside your hungry tum. Like Connie and Mellors, embrace the fertile forest floor and all it has to offer ... for nothing tastes as good as forbidden fruit, whether it's this succulent scattering of bounteous berries, over lush layers of sumptuous sponge - or the banned body of the glorious gamekeeper.

Serves 8–10

200g/7oz soft butter, plus extra for greasing
200g/7oz caster sugar
4 eggs, lightly beaten
200g/7oz self-raising flour
1 tsp baking powder

For the filling
400ml/14fl oz double cream
2 tbsp icing sugar, plus extra to dust
6 tbsp blackcurrant jam
300g/11oz frozen forest fruits, defrosted and drained

1. Heat the oven to 190C/375F/gas 5 and grease and line the bases of two 20cm (8in) round cake tins with baking paper. Put all the cake ingredients into a bowl and beat until smooth.

2. Divide the mixture between the cake tins, smooth the surface with the back of a spoon, then bake for 20–25 minutes or until golden and a skewer inserted into the centre comes out clean. Allow to cool in the tin for a few minutes then transfer to a wire rack to cool completely.

3. To assemble the cakes, whip the cream and icing sugar to soft peaks then set aside. Once the cakes are cool, cut each one in half horizontally, choose the neatest layer to go on the top and set it aside. Put the bottom layer on a serving plate, then spread with 2 tablespoons of jam, one-third of the whipped cream and one-third of the fruit. Repeat with the other two cakes. Finally, top the stack with your chosen cake layer and dust generously with icing sugar.

JANE ÉCLAIR

COFFEE ÉCLAIRS WITH RUM AND VANILLA CREAM

Take one orphaned egg, a white floury ghost story, a school run by a man with morals as slippery as butter and one pinch of salted tears. Once baked by education, introduce a dark, tempting hero. And behold: a happy-ever-after union of sensual chocolate and virgin choux pastry: the first as rich as Rochester; the latter light as Eyre.

But there's a twist … hidden at the heart of these mysterious melting mouthfuls lies a Jamaican-flavoured secret, bursting with insane levels of taste. An explosive combination that's blindingly good. Reader, I masticated it.

Makes 10 éclairs

85g/3oz butter, diced
140g/5oz plain flour, sifted
3 eggs, lightly beaten

For the filling
2 tbsp dark rum
600ml/1 pint double cream
1 tsp vanilla extract

For the topping
½ tsp instant coffee powder
1 tbsp dark rum
140g/5oz icing sugar
1 tsp vanilla extract

Tip
omit the rum for a classic love story without the mad first wife.

1. Heat the oven to 200C/400F/gas 6. Gently heat the butter in a medium-sized pan with 225ml (8fl oz) water until melted, then bring to the boil. Remove from the heat and beat in the flour to a shiny dough that leaves the pan sides. Cool in a bowl for 5 minutes.

2. Gradually add the eggs and beat to a smooth dough that falls reluctantly from the spoon. Pile into a piping bag fitted with a 1.5cm (½in) round nozzle and allow to rest for 5 minutes.

3. Line baking trays with baking paper, then pipe ten thick, 12cm (5in) sausages. Bake for 25 minutes until golden and crisp. Split each in half lengthways then put them cut side up, in pairs, on the trays and return to the oven for 5 minutes to dry out and crisp up. Transfer to a wire rack to cool.

4. Meanwhile, make the filling and topping. Put the rum, cream and vanilla extract in a large bowl and whip to soft peaks. Set aside. Dissolve the coffee in the rum, then stir into the icing sugar and vanilla to make a thick, spreadable icing. Spread generously over the éclair tops. Pile the rum cream into a piping bag fitted with a 1cm (½in) round nozzle and pipe it onto the éclair bottom. Top with the iced half and eat immediately or chill until ready to serve.

WHOOPIE PIES & PREJUDICE

SALTED-CARAMEL WHOOPIE PIES

I t is a truth universally acknowledged that a single reader in possession of a good appetite must be in want of a knife ... with which to slice up these delicious salted caramel cakes. Tastier than the vision of Mr Darcy emerging dripping wet from a country lake, these whoopie pies combine two feisty yet clearly meant-to-be-together halves into one delicious marriage of moreishness.

Makes 10 whoopie pies

300g/11oz self-raising flour
1½ tsp bicarbonate of soda
175g/6oz soft light brown sugar
¼ tsp sea salt, plus extra to serve
1 egg, lightly beaten
75g/2½oz sunflower oil, plus extra for greasing
150ml/¼ pint fat-free natural yogurt
75ml/2½fl oz milk
1 tsp vanilla extract

For the salted caramel
85g/3oz butter, diced
100g/4oz soft light brown sugar
1 tsp vanilla extract
¼ tsp sea salt
200ml/7fl oz double cream

1. First make the salted caramel filling. Put the butter, sugar, vanilla, salt and cream into a large saucepan over a medium heat. Stir continuously until the butter melts and the sugar dissolves. Bring the mixture to the boil and cook for 1 minute or until the sauce thickens slightly. Remove from the heat and allow to cool completely until thick and spreadable.

2. Heat the oven to 180C/350F/gas 4 and line a couple of baking trays with baking paper.

3. Mix the flour, bicarbonate of soda, sugar and salt in a big bowl. In another bowl whisk together the egg, oil, yogurt, milk and vanilla extract. Pour the wet ingredients into the dry and stir to combine.

4. Drop 20 tablespoons of mixture onto the prepared trays, leaving plenty of space for spreading. Bake for 12 minutes or until firm to touch. Allow to cool for a few minutes then transfer to a wire rack to cool completely.

5. Sandwich 2 cakes with caramel sauce, sprinkle with a little more salt and serve.

ROMANTIC PICNIC

Find a secluded spot, throw off your shoes, sit back with your loved one and enjoy the fruits of your kitchen labour. If the weather isn't playing the game but romance is in the air, enjoy a carpet picnic in the comfort of your own home.

~~~~~~

LOLI-POP-ITA

Chocolate bowl with dipped fruits (see page 28)

—

WHOOPIE PIES & PREJUDICE

Salted-caramel whoopie pies (see page 21)

—

ROULADE & JULIET

Almond, apricot and rose roulade (see page 144)

~~~~~~

Serve with chilled sparkling wine with sliced strawberries.

WUTHERING BITES

TRADITIONAL YORKSHIRE PARKIN

~~~~~~~

P arkin. Traditional Yorkshire fare. One can almost taste the windswept moors in every bite. Like Heathcliff's revenge, this is a dish best served cold, perhaps with a cup of Brontë on the side. Not for a Yorkshire pudding the swirls and twirls of elaborate embellishment - this is a bake of little visible delight, but necessary.

Yet one Wuthering Bite is never enough ... you may well find yourself sneaking around late at night, making your way to the closed cake tin with a dastardly plan to prise it open, crying out to its stiffened lid: 'Let me in! Oh, let me in ... '

Serves 6–8

100g/4oz butter, plus extra for greasing

175g/5oz self-raising flour

85g/3oz medium oatmeal

1 tbsp ground ginger

1 tsp mixed spice

85g/3oz raisins

½ tsp bicarbonate of soda

5 tbsp golden syrup

4 tbsp black treacle

75g/2½oz soft light brown sugar

1 egg, lightly beaten

1. Heat the oven to 160C/325F/gas 3. Grease and line the sides and base of a 20cm (8in) round cake tin with baking paper.

2. Combine the flour, oatmeal, spices, raisins and bicarbonate of soda in a bowl and set aside.

3. Put the butter, syrup, treacle and sugar in a small pan. Heat gently, stirring occasionally to combine, until the sugar has melted. Remove from the heat and allow to cool for a few minutes before stirring in the egg. Pour the wet ingredients into the dry and stir to combine. Allow to stand for 5 minutes.

4. Pour the mixture into the cake tin. Bake for 50–60 minutes or until the cake feels firm and is dark brown in colour. Leave to cool in the tin, then remove and wrap in baking paper and store in a cake tin until ready to serve. Parkin gets more sticky and delicious with age, so try and leave it for a couple of days before slicing and serving with a strong cup of tea.

MANSFIELD TART

RASPBERRY AND VANILLA CUSTARD TART

~~~~~~

Relish the romance of the Regency era and transport yourself – just like Fanny Price – to a hitherto unknown world of plush desserts filled with ingénue-like vanilla custard and a sprinkling of somewhat more rakish raspberries. You'll need no Persuasion to enjoy this delicate and delicious dessert: it makes perfect Sense (and Sensibility) to indulge yourself.

Fanny may not be everyone's cup of tea, but there'll be nothing but harmony and happy endings at the dinner table upon the serving of this particular pudding. Even Mrs Norris couldn't quibble with that.

Serves 6

For the pastry

175g/6oz plain flour, plus extra for dusting

140g/5oz cold butter, diced

25g/1oz caster sugar

1 tsp vanilla extract

zest of 1 orange

1 egg yolk

1. To make the pastry, sift the flour into a bowl and rub in the butter with your fingertips. Add the sugar, vanilla and orange zest and then, using a round-bladed knife, stir in the egg yolk together with 2–3 teaspoons of cold water to form a stiff dough. Knead the pastry dough briefly until smooth, then wrap in cling film and chill in the fridge for 20 minutes.

2. Heat the oven to 180C/350F/gas 4. Roll out the pastry on a floured work surface to 5mm (¼ in) thick then carefully transfer to a 20cm (8in) round, loose-bottomed, fluted flan tin set on a baking sheet. Scrunch up a piece of baking paper, fill it with baking beans then blind-bake the pastry case for 15 minutes. Lift out the paper and beans, return the pastry case to the oven and cook for a further 10 minutes or until the pastry is pale golden.

For the vanilla custard
2 whole eggs, plus 2 yolks
50g/2oz caster sugar
½ vanilla pod, seeds scraped
450ml/16fl oz single cream

To finish
175g/6oz raspberries
1 tbsp caster sugar

3. To make the custard filling, beat the whole eggs, egg yolks and sugar in a bowl. Set aside. Put the vanilla pod and seeds in a small pan with the cream and heat to just below boiling point. Gradually pour the hot cream onto the egg mixture, whisking constantly, then strain the custard into the pastry case.

4. Lower the oven temperature to 150C/300F/gas 2. Return the filled tart to the oven and bake for 45 minutes or until the custard is set but with a slight wobble. Remove from the oven and leave to cool.

5. Toss the raspberries in the sugar, leave to stand for 5 minutes then pile on top of the tart to serve.

LOVE IN THE TIME OF PAVLOVA

COCONUT PAVLOVA WITH PASSION FRUIT SAUCE

G abriel García Márquez's classic Caribbean tale of love and fidelity lives on in every bite of this exotic tropical-flavoured pavlova, served with an aptly named passion fruit sauce as an ambrosial addition to the love story. Like Florentino and Fermina, this coconut concoction is a story of contrasting personalities, in which the sweetness of the coconut somehow gels with the tartness of the fruit. All topped, of course, with the taste of bitter almonds.

Serves 6–8

4 egg whites

200g/7oz caster sugar

1 tsp vanilla extract

1 tsp white wine vinegar

1 tsp cornflour

50g/2oz toasted, shaved coconut

300ml/½ pint double cream, lightly whipped

1 ripe mango, peeled and chopped

For the passion fruit sauce

100g/4oz caster sugar

1. Heat the oven to 140C/275F/gas 1. Draw a rough 23cm (9in) circle on a piece of baking paper, flip it over and set on a baking sheet.

2. Whisk the egg whites in a large clean bowl until they form stiff peaks. Gradually add the sugar, whisking all the time and making sure it is fully incorporated after each addition. Continue to whisk until you have thick, glossy meringue. Make a paste with the vanilla extract, white wine vinegar and cornflour, then whisk it into the meringues, folding in two-thirds of the coconut.

3. Use a large metal spoon to dollop the mixture onto the paper. Gently swirl and spread out the meringue to fill the circle, making a slight dip in the centre. Scatter with the remaining coconut and bake in the oven for 1 hour. The pavlova should be slightly puffy, light golden and firm to the touch. Turn off the oven, open the door slightly and leave the pavlova inside until it is completely cool.

4 passion fruit, pulp and seeds scooped out

zest and juice of 1 lime

handful of almonds, to decorate

good-quality vanilla ice cream, to serve

4. Meanwhile, make the passion fruit sauce. Put the sugar, passion fruit pulp and seeds, lime juice and zest into a small pan with 75ml (2½fl oz) water. Heat gently until the sugar dissolves, then increase the heat and bubble for 3–4 minutes or until the sauce is syrupy. Remove from the heat and allow to cool.

5. To serve, put the pavlova on a big plate, spoon over the lightly whipped cream, top with the mango, pour over the passion fruit sauce and sprinkle with almonds. Cut the pavlova into generous wedges and serve each with a scoop of vanilla ice cream.

LOLI-POP-ITA

CHOCOLATE BOWL WITH DIPPED FRUITS

L ol-li-pop-i-ta. Roll it around your tongue and devour the dipped fruits, the fruits of my loins. Savour the sensation of the forbidden fruit as it fornicates in the dark depths of the chocolate bowl, dripping in deliciously damp molten squares of the finest chocolate. Raise it to your lips. Deflower each mouthful, dip by dip by dip. Satiate your cravings…

And Lo, by the end of your lavish feast, have you been taken in by the cool, persuasive narration of Humbert Humbert, or succumbed to the sensual allure of underage afters?

Serves 6–8

250g/9oz plain chocolate, roughly chopped

250g/9oz milk chocolate, roughly chopped

2 tbsp golden syrup

300ml/½ pint double cream

100ml/3½fl oz milk

For dipping

½ pineapple, peeled and cut into chunks

3 small bananas, peeled and cut into chunks

300g/11oz strawberries, hulled

150g bag marshmallows

cocktail sticks or skewers

1. Put all the chocolate into a large heatproof bowl set over a pan of barely simmering water along with the syrup, double cream and milk. Once the chocolate starts to melt, stir to combine until you have a smooth, velvety, chocolate sauce.

2. Spear the fruit pieces and marshmallows with cocktail sticks and place them on serving plates. Divide the molten chocolate sauce between pretty teacups and serve alongside the fruits and marshmallows.

'There was something strange in my sensations, something indescribably sweet ... and the thought, in that moment, braced and delighted me.'
—
Robert Louis Stevenson,
The Strange Case of Dr Jekyll & Mr Hyde

THRILLERS, CRIME & HORROR

MURDER ON THE ORIENT ESPRESSO CAKES

ESPRESSO CAKES WITH MOCHA CUSTARD AND CREAM

B aked goods are not often associated with murky murders, but these deliciously dark cakes, opulently finished with traces of gold leaf, are so good that everyone would kill for a taste.

The secret identity of the killer ingredient is fast revealed by the little Belgian chocolate detective – in a room, with all suspects gathered – as a dusting of the richest espresso powder. How very continental.

All aboard the luxurious Orient Espresso cake train for the culinary ride of your life. You will not need your little grey cells – or even Poirot himself – to tell you that *these* cakes are to die for.

Makes 6 cakes

3 eggs
75g/2½oz soft light brown sugar
75g/2½oz plain flour

For the mocha custard
50g/2oz caster sugar
4 tsp cornflour
2 egg yolks

1. Heat the oven to 200C/400F/gas 6. Grease and line a 33 x 23cm (13 x 9in) Swiss roll tin with baking paper. Put the eggs and sugar in a large heatproof bowl over a pan of barely simmering water and whisk until the mixture is thick enough to leave a trail on the surface when the whisk is lifted – about 8 minutes. Remove the bowl from the pan and whisk until cooled.

2. Sift the flour into the egg mixture and use a metal spoon to fold it in. Tip the cake mixture into the tin and smooth the surface with the back of a spoon. Bake for 10–12 minutes until well risen and just firm. Remove from the oven and tip out on to a large piece of baking paper, peel off the original paper and allow to cool.

½ tsp vanilla extract

200ml/7fl oz milk

100ml/3½fl oz double cream

2 tbsp instant espresso powder

25g/1oz chocolate-coated coffee beans, finely chopped, plus extra to decorate

To assemble

150ml/¼ pint double cream

cocoa powder, to dust

edible gold leaf (optional)

3. To make the custard, place the sugar, cornflour, egg yolks, vanilla extract and a little of the milk in a bowl and beat until smooth. Put the rest of the milk, the cream and espresso powder in a pan and bring to the boil. Remove from the heat and gradually pour over the custard mixture, stirring until smooth. Return to the heat and cook, stirring, for 2–3 minutes until thickened. Stir in the chopped coffee beans. Transfer to a bowl, cover the surface with cling film and allow to cool.

4. Whip the double cream to soft peaks and set aside.

5. To assemble the cakes, use a 6cm (2.5in) round cutter to cut out 12 rounds from the sponge. Spoon a little custard onto half of the rounds, then top with the remaining sponges. Dollop a spoon of whipped cream on top, dust generously with cocoa powder then sprinkle with the remaining chocolate coffee beans. To make this extra special, dust a little gold leaf on top of the cakes and serve on your prettiest plates with a little cake fork.

THE PICTURE OF DORIAN SOUFFLÉ

MANDARIN SOUFFLÉ

~~~~~~~

L ike many things, this dish is best served straight from the oven, while its youthful vigour and good looks show no sign of failing, and when it's quite the picture of culinary health. Be warned, though, the moment you stab at it with a silver spoon or a well-aimed pastry fork, its power ceases and its puffed-up performance of perfection meets its end … Beneath the surface, the sultry taste of sinful sweetened fruits awaits, all wickedness and depravity laid on for all to see. I predict you'll go Wilde for it.

Serves 4

large knob of butter

50g/2oz golden caster sugar

1 x 312g can mandarin segments, drained

150ml/¼ pint ready-made custard

1 tbsp cornflour

zest of 2 mandarins

4 egg whites

1. Heat the oven to 180C/350F/gas 4 and put a baking sheet in the oven to heat up. Grease four 150ml ramekins with butter, then dust them with a tablespoon of the caster sugar, tipping out any excess.

2. Divide the mandarin segments between the ramekins, being careful not to knock the sugar from the edge of the dishes. Set aside.

3. Mix the custard with the cornflour and mandarin zest until combined. In another, clean, bowl, whisk the egg whites until they reach stiff peaks. Gradually add in the remaining caster sugar and whisk after each addition to dissolve the sugar. Continue whisking until the egg whites are very stiff and shiny. Add a quarter of the egg white to the custard mixture to loosen, then fold in the remaining egg whites.

4. Remove the baking sheet from the oven, sit the ramekins on top, and then, working quickly, divide the mixture between the dishes. Run a finger around the edge of each dish then bake them for 15 minutes, or until risen and golden on top. Serve immediately.

DORIAN SOUFFLÉ

THE TALENTED MR RASPBERRY RIPPLE

RASPBERRY RIPPLE ICE CREAM

T he icy-cold heart of this delicious ice cream perfectly mirrors the immoral centre of Mr Tom Ripley himself. Have yourself a double scoop – can you tell the two apart? Set amid the splendour of Italy, in the spiritual and literal home of ice cream, this is a chilling tale of intertwining identities and deceptive doppelgangers. Can you even be sure that the jewelled red coulis rippling through the ice cream is made from raspberries … ?

Serves 4–6

1 vanilla pod, split
300ml/½ pint milk
3 egg yolks
75g/2½oz caster sugar
300ml/½ pint double cream

For the raspberry ripple
50g/2oz caster sugar
200g/7oz raspberries

1. Put the vanilla pod in a pan with the milk and heat to just boiling point. Remove from the heat and set aside for 20 minutes to infuse.

2. Whisk the egg yolks and sugar together in a large bowl until thick and creamy. Remove the vanilla pod from the milk and gradually pour the hot milk into the eggs and sugar, whisking all the while. Strain the mixture back into the pan and cook over a low heat, stirring constantly, until thick enough to coat the back of a wooden spoon. Do not allow the mixture to boil. Pour the custard into a clean bowl and allow to cool.

3. Meanwhile, make the raspberry ripple. Put the sugar in a small pan with 2 tablespoons of water, heat gently, stirring constantly until the sugar has dissolved and the liquid is syrupy. Remove from the heat, tip in the raspberries and mash with a fork. Pass the fruit through a sieve, discard the seeds and allow the pulp to cool.

4. Pour the cooled custard into an ice-cream maker and churn until almost frozen, then decant into a freezerproof container and swirl through the cold raspberry sauce using a metal skewer. Freeze for 2 hours, or until solid. If you don't have an ice-cream maker, pour the mixture into a freezerproof container and freeze for 1 hour, then give it a good whisk to break up the ice crystals and freeze for another hour. Repeat until the ice cream starts to solidify.

5. Allow the ice cream to soften slightly at room temperature before serving.

THE STRANGE CAKE OF DR JELLY & MR H'ICE CREAM

RASPBERRY JELLY AND LEMON ICE CREAM CAKE

AIM: To create a strange cake that's so good it's bad.

HYPOTHESIS: The sharp lemon ice cream will be contained by the innocent vanilla sponge cake and a respectable raspberry jelly.

METHOD: See detailed experiment notes below.

RESULTS: While at first the strange cake presented an upright tower of clearly delineated strata, each with its own personality, before too long the tart tang of the lemon ice cream began to assert itself. Bit by bit it melted and oozed through the vanilla sponge, melding with the jelly until it was unclear where one ended and the other began. The unstoppable molten stream became uncontrollable. Still, it was delicious – and vendors of such a dish will surely make a killing.

CONCLUSION: Better than a banana split (personality).

Serves 6–8

200g/7oz soft butter
200g/7oz caster sugar
200g/7oz self-raising flour
1 tsp baking powder
4 eggs
zest of 2 lemons

1. First prepare the jelly and ice-cream filling. Line a 20cm (8in) round cake tin with cling film. Spread the ice cream in the tin in an even layer, swirl through 2 tablespoons of the lemon curd and place in the freezer.

2. Meanwhile, make up the jelly by dissolving it in 150ml (¼ pint) boiling water. Place in the fridge and allow to cool completely, but do not let it set. Once cold, remove the ice cream from the freezer, pour the jelly liquid on top of the ice cream layer, dot over the raspberries and return to the freezer for at least 1 hour or until the jelly is completely set.

For the filling

½ x 500ml tub good-quality vanilla ice cream, slightly softened

3 tbsp lemon curd

½ x 135g packet raspberry flavoured jelly

handful of raspberries, plus extra to serve (optional)

icing sugar, to serve

3. Now make the cakes. Heat the oven to 190C/350F/gas 5. Grease and line two 20cm (8in) round cake tins with baking paper. Put the butter, sugar, flour, baking powder, eggs and lemon zest in a large bowl and beat until smooth.

4. Divide the mixture between the tins, smooth the surface and bake for 20 minutes or until golden, risen and springy to the touch. Leave to cool in the tin for a few minutes, then transfer to a wire rack to cool completely.

5. To assemble the cake, spread the top of one cake and the bottom of the other with lemon curd. Remove the jelly and ice cream from the freezer, flip the cake tin jelly-side down onto the cake spread with lemon curd. Peel off the cling film from the ice cream and top with the other cake, curd-side down. Dust the top generously with icing sugar, slice into wedges and serve immediately with extra raspberries, if you like.

THE HOUND OF THE (BAKED) ALASKA-VILLES

BAKED ALASKA

~~~

T ake a good long look at the dish before you, Dr Watson. What do you see? 'Steaming peaks of baked meringue: a hot pudding straight from the oven?' Wrong, my friend, wrong. You see, but you do not observe. You know my methods, my dear Watson, and they may well be founded upon 'the observation of trifles', but in this case we are looking not at a trifle, but at a Baked Alaska!

Cut into it. See below the surface. This is no mere hot pudding, but an ice-cream dish masquerading as meringue! I have told you before, that when you have eliminated the impossible, whatever remains, however improbable, must be the truth. The truth in this particular, peculiar case is that the detective from Baker Street has debunked a delicious and science-defying baked good. *Elementary*.

Serves 6–8

100g/4oz butter, softened, plus extra for greasing
100g/4oz caster sugar
2 eggs, lightly beaten
1 tsp vanilla extract
100g/4oz self-raising flour
>

1. Heat the oven to 180C/350F/gas 4. Grease and line the base of a 20cm (8in) round cake tin with baking paper. Beat the butter and sugar together until pale and creamy, then gradually add the eggs and vanilla extract, beating after each addition. Fold the flour into the wet ingredients.

2. Pile the mixture into the cake tin and smooth the surface. Bake for 20–25 minutes until cooked and golden. Allow to cool in the tin for a few minutes then transfer to a wire rack to cool completely.

>

THE HOUND OF THE (BAKED) ALASKA-VILLES
(cont.)

For the filling

2 tbsp of your favourite jam

500ml/18fl oz tub vanilla or raspberry ice cream

4 egg whites

200g/7oz caster sugar

3. Place the cake on a baking tray and spread with jam, then set aside. Remove the ice cream from the freezer and run a blunt knife round the edge to loosen it. Tip it out onto a chopping board and flatten it slightly with the palm your hand so that it spreads out at the base and is lower in height. Transfer the ice cream to the cake and put back in the freezer for an hour or until solid.

4. Heat the oven to 220C/425F/gas 7. Whisk the egg whites in a large clean bowl until stiff, then gradually add the sugar, continuing to whisk between each addition until firm and very glossy. Remove the ice-cream-topped cake from the freezer. Spread the meringue evenly all over the ice cream and cake – make sure you have no gaps. Use a fork to make a swirly pattern over the surface. Bake for 6–8 minutes, or until lightly golden, then serve immediately.

MURDER MYSTERY

*These cakes will certainly keep you guessing.
Whose blood has been spilled and used to
make the bright red jelly?*

———

MURDER ON THE
ORIENT ESPRESSO CAKES

Espresso cakes with mocha custard and cream (see page 32)

—

THE STRANGE CAKE OF
DR JELLY & MR H'ICE CREAM

Raspberry jelly and lemon ice cream cake (see page 38)

—

KEY LIME & PUNISHMENT

Boozy key lime pie (see page 48)

———

*Serve with a poisonous-looking cocktail …
Pour 8 shots of Fernet Branca over ice into
8 tumblers and top each with a measure of
crème de menthe. Sip vigilantly.*

THE PIE WHO LOVED ME

BRAMLEY APPLE AND BLACKBERRY PIE

T his is pie. Apple pie. Neither shaken nor stirred, but baked and sliced – and in possession of a licence to thrill. You don't need to be James Bond on Her Majesty's Secret Service to work out that this is a dish you can't say (Dr) no to. In fact, with its luscious Bramley-apple-and-blackberry filling, it's so delicious you'll think you've died and gone to double-oh-heaven.

If the one slice is not enough, why not have another? After all, you only live twice …

Serves 8

500g pack ready-made short-crust pastry

flour, for dusting

50g/2oz caster sugar, plus extra to sprinkle

50g/2oz soft dark brown sugar

1 tbsp plain flour

good scraping of nutmeg

½ tsp ground cinnamon

zest and juice of 1 orange

500g/1lb 2oz Bramley apples, peeled, cored and sliced

200g/7oz blackberries

50g/2oz sultanas

25g/1oz butter, chopped into small cubes

splash of milk, to glaze

1. Roll out two-thirds of the pastry on a lightly floured work surface and use to line a 23cm (9in) pie plate. Chill for 30 minutes, along with the remaining pastry.

2. Combine the sugars, flour, spices and orange zest, then sprinkle a little of this onto the pastry case. Cover with half the sliced apples and half the blackberries, then sprinkle over half the sultanas and half of the remaining sugar mix. Repeat using all the apples, sultanas and sugar, sprinkle with orange juice and dot with butter. Brush the edge with a little milk.

3. Heat the oven to 190C/375F/gas 5. Roll out the remaining pastry and cover the pie filling, pressing the edges together to seal. Slash the middle of the pastry lid a couple of times to allow steam to escape while baking. Brush the top of the pie with milk, dust with caster sugar and bake for 40–45 minutes until the fruit is tender and the top is golden brown. Allow to stand for a few minutes before serving with custard or cream, if you like.

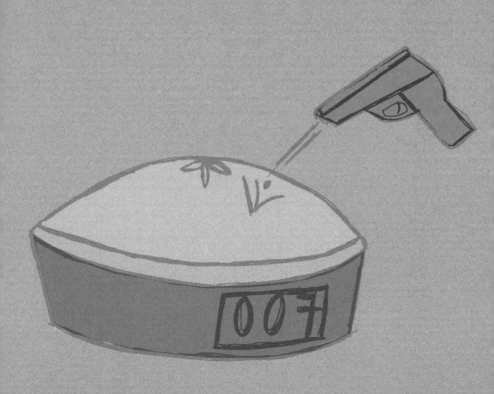

THE WOMAN IN BLACK FOREST GÂTEAU

BLACK FOREST GÂTEAU

〜〜〜

Feast your eyes on the Woman in Black Forest Gâteau with no fear of repercussions. You'll want every one of your Nine Lives (Causeway) to enjoy the thick, dark sweetness of this glorious gâteau. That said, like Arthur Kipps, you may well be haunted long after the event – if only by the memory of the bitter chocolate, juicy cherries and marsh-like gooeyness that make up every mouthful.

Serves 8–10

100g/4oz plain chocolate
175g/6oz butter, softened
300g/11oz soft dark brown sugar
3 eggs, lightly beaten
300g/11oz plain flour
1 tsp bicarbonate of soda
2 tsp baking powder
150ml/¼ pint sour cream

1. Heat the oven to 190C/350F/gas 5. Grease and line the base of three 20cm (8in) round cake tins with baking paper. Chop 75g (3oz) of chocolate and put in a small pan with 150ml (¼ pint) water, heat gently until melted, stir to combine, then remove from the heat and allow to cool.

2. Beat the butter and sugar with an electric whisk until pale and fluffy then gradually add the eggs. Mix together the flour, bicarbonate of soda and baking powder in a large bowl and make a well in the centre, then add the wet ingredients and stir to combine. Fold in the melted chocolate and sour cream until combined then divide between the prepared tins. Smooth the surface with the back of a spoon and bake for 25–30 minutes, or until a skewer inserted into the centre comes out clean. Allow to cool in the tins for a few minutes, then transfer to a wire rack to cool completely.

For the filling

425g can cherries in light
syrup, drained and syrup
reserved

1 tbsp cornflour

3 tbsp kirsch or brandy

600ml/1 pint double cream

handful fresh cherries, to
decorate

3. Meanwhile, make the filling. Use a little of the reserved cherry syrup to make a paste with the cornflour. Pour the remaining cherry syrup into a small pan and heat until boiling, add the cornflour paste, reduce the heat and cook for 2 minutes or until the syrup is thick and glossy. Remove from the heat and fold through the drained cherries. Set aside to cool.

4. Drizzle the kirsch or brandy over the cakes then set aside to allow it to soak in. Whip the cream to soft peaks and spoon it over the tops of the cakes, divide the saucy cherries between two of the cakes then sandwich them together. Place the remaining cake on top and curl the remaining chocolate over the top with a potato peeler. Decorate with fresh cherries and chill until ready to serve.

KEY LIME & PUNISHMENT

BOOZY KEY LIME PIE

~~~

B oth book and bake here hail from the nineteenth century, but in a time-travelling twist, the classic Florida Keys dish gets some Russian va-va-voom with the addition of some not-so-classic lime-flavoured vodka. Marmeladov, the drunkard, would be sure to approve.

While Dostoyevsky's novel ruminates on the power of a guilty conscience, none is necessary when consuming this fabulously fruity dessert, which packs a punch through the zest of its limes rather than the violence of its protagonists. Murderously tasty.

Serves 8

300g/11oz digestive biscuits
2 tbsp caster sugar
100g/4oz butter, melted

For the filling
3 egg yolks
397g can condensed milk
zest and juice of 4 limes
1 tablespoon vodka (lime-flavoured is even better)

For the topping
300ml/½ pint double cream
3 tbsp vodka (lime-flavoured is even better)
2 tbsp icing sugar
zest and juice of 1 lime

1. Heat the oven to 160C/325F/gas 3. Grease and line the base of a 22cm (9in) springform cake tin or loose-bottomed tart tin with baking paper. Put the biscuits into a plastic bag and bash with a rolling pin to fine crumbs. Tip into a bowl and combine with the sugar and melted butter. Spread the crumbs evenly over the base of the tin and about 3cm (1in) up the sides. Place on a baking sheet and cook for 10 minutes. Allow to cool.

2. In a large bowl, whisk the egg yolks until pale, fluffy and doubled in volume. Continue to whisk for about 5 minutes, gradually adding the condensed milk, lime juice and zest and vodka – the mix should be pale and creamy. Carefully pour onto the cooled biscuit base. Transfer to the oven and cook for 20 minutes, or until the filling is set but with a slight wobble. Remove and allow to cool completely. Chill until required.

3. When ready to serve, put the cream, vodka, icing sugar and lime juice in a large bowl and whisk to soft peaks. Remove the pie from the fridge, pile over the flavoured cream, sprinkle with lime zest and serve with an ice-cold shot of vodka, if you like.

BRIGHTON ROCK 'N' ROLL

BRIGHTON ROCK AND RASPBERRY SWISS ROLL

~~~~~~

Your friends will be (Graham) Greene with envy when you produce this thrillingly good Brighton Rock 'n' Roll. Pinkie in colour and simultaneously sweet and Spicer, with a unique topping of traditional crunchy Brighton rock, just one slice will make you feel Hale and hearty. Ida even bet you'll be the most popular member of your gang – or at least a-pier that way while stocks last …

Serves 6–8

25g/1oz butter, melted, plus extra for greasing
3 eggs
100g/4oz caster sugar
red food colouring paste
100g/4oz plain flour

For the filling

2 small sticks of Brighton rock, bashed to little nuggets
100g/4oz raspberries
1 tbsp icing sugar
200ml/7fl oz double cream

>

1. Heat the oven to 200C/400F/gas 6 Grease and line a 20 x 30cm (8 x 12in) baking tin with baking paper. Put the eggs, sugar and a little food colouring paste in a large bowl and beat with an electric whisk for 8–10 minutes, until the mixture is pale, thick, and the whisk leaves a 'ribbon' trail when lifted from the egg mix.

2. Sift half the flour over the whisked eggs and sugar, and then gently fold it into the egg. Sift in the remaining flour and fold in. Drizzle the melted butter around the edge of the bowl and fold in.

3. Pour the batter into the tin and smooth the surface with the back of a spoon. Bake for 10–12 minutes or until springy to the touch. Remove from the oven and allow to cool for a few minutes.

>

BRIGHTON
ROCK 'N' ROLL
(cont.)

4. Meanwhile, lay a large piece of baking paper on a flat surface, sprinkle over half of the crushed rock, then tip the sponge directly on top of it. Peel the original baking paper off the sponge. Starting with the longest end furthest from you, roll the sponge up to form a long roll. Twist the ends of the paper to secure and set aside to cool completely.

5. To make the filling, put the raspberries in a bowl with the icing sugar, squash with a fork to break up the berries and let stand for a few minutes until the raspberries become a bit saucy. Whip the cream to soft peaks then fold through most of the remaining rock, saving a little for patching the surface.

6. Unwrap the pink sponge base, leaving it on the baking paper. Spread over the raspberries and the rock cream. Re-roll, using the baking paper to help you. Carefully transfer the roll to a plate, seam side down, and remove the baking paper, then patch up any cracks with the reserved rock. Cut into slices and serve.

'If the purpose of food is nourishment and the purpose of marriage is the family, the whole question resolves itself into not eating more than one can digest.'

—

Leo Tolstoy, *War & Peace*

HISTORICAL
& WAR

FOR WHOM THE BELL TUILES

TUILES WITH CHOCOLATE-CHILLI SAUCE

~~~~~~

I tell you in Ernest: these terrific tuiles are explosively enticing. Packed full of Spanish savour and red-hot chilli, they bring a bang to the palate that Robert Jordan would have loved to unleash on the Franco fascists at the heart of the Spanish Civil War. Perfect for bridging the gap between the main course and coffee, these dinner-party delights are the guerrillas of gastronomy, putting the dynamite back into dining.

Serves 6–8

2 egg whites
100g/4oz caster sugar
50g/2oz plain flour
50g/2oz butter, melted and cooled

1. Draw a bell shape on a piece of paper about 7cm (3in) high and 6cm (2.5in) wide, or a 7cm (3in) diameter circle. Tape the paper to the piece of plastic and cut around the shape. Discard the cut-out plastic shape and the paper, keeping the plastic stencil.

2. Heat the oven to 180C/350F/gas 4. Line a couple of baking trays with non-stick baking paper. Put the egg whites into a clean bowl with a pinch of salt and whisk lightly with a fork until foamy. Add the sugar and continue to whisk for a minute. Tip in the flour and stir to combine, then add the melted butter to create a batter.

3. Lay your stencil on top of the baking paper, dollop a teaspoon of batter into the centre then smooth out with a pallet knife to fill the space. Carefully lift the stencil to reveal the shape. Continue to do this until you have 3–4 tuiles on each baking sheet.

For the chocolate-chilli sauce

150g/4½ oz plain chocolate, roughly chopped

2 tbsp golden syrup

knob of butter

¼ tsp chilli flakes

chocolate ice cream, to serve

You will need a 10 x 10cm (4 x 4in) piece of plastic – an old take-away lid is perfect – to make a tuile stencil

4. Bake for 5–7 minutes, until golden at the edges. Remove from the oven and cool for a few minutes on the tray, then carefully transfer to a wire rack to cool completely.

5. To make the chocolate-chilli sauce, put the chocolate, golden syrup, butter, chilli flakes and 100ml (3½ fl oz) water in a bowl set over a pan of barely simmering water. Stir until the chocolate has melted and the sauce is smooth and glossy. Remove from the heat, pour into little serving glasses and serve with the tuiles and a scoop of chocolate ice cream.

ALONE IN BERLINER

CUSTARD-FILLED DOUGHNUTS

~~~~~

B erliners may at first appear a submissive sort of pudding; soft to the touch, and yielding. Yet their sweet filling reveals startling hidden depths. For these delicious doughnuts – like the townsfolk themselves – possess ingredients that will surprise you. Turns out, not all Berliners are cowardly as custard, after all …

Makes 12

225ml/8fl oz milk
50g/2oz butter, diced
2 eggs, lightly beaten
500g/1lb 2oz strong white bread flour, plus extra for dusting
50g/2oz caster sugar
1 x 7g sachet dried fast-action yeast

1. Heat the milk in a small pan to just below boiling point. Remove from the heat, add the butter and swirl the pan to melt it. Leave to cool for about 5 minutes until you can comfortably dip your little finger into the liquid, then stir in the eggs.

2. Put the flour, sugar and yeast into a large mixing bowl and stir to combine, then add a pinch of salt. Make a well in the centre of the flour and gradually pour in the milk and butter mixture, stirring to form a soft, slightly sticky dough. Tip the dough onto a lightly floured work surface and knead for 10 minutes or until it is soft and shiny. Place the dough into a lightly greased bowl, cover with a clean cloth and leave to stand in a warm spot until doubled in size – about 1 hour.

3. Meanwhile, make the filling. Gently heat the milk to just below boiling point. In a separate bowl, mix the egg yolks, sugar, cornflour and the vanilla seeds until combined. Remove the milk from the heat and gradually add to the yolk mixture, stirring all the time. Pour the mixture back into the pan and cook over a medium heat for about 5 minutes, stirring continuously, until smooth and thick.

For the filling
200ml/7fl oz milk
3 egg yolks
50g/2oz caster sugar
1 tbsp cornflour
1 vanilla pod, seeds scraped
100ml/3½fl oz double cream

To finish
1 litre/1¾ pints sunflower oil
100g/4oz caster sugar

4. Remove from the heat, tip into a bowl, cover the surface with cling film and allow to cool completely. Whip the cream to soft peaks then fold through the cold custard. Cover and chill until required.

5. Tip out the dough onto a floured work surface and knead briefly to get rid of any air bubbles. Flatten the dough to a 2cm (1in) thickness. Use a 7cm (3in) round cutter to stamp out the dough, or cut it into 12 equal parts with a knife and shape these into neat balls. Transfer to two baking trays lined with baking paper, leaving a 5cm (2in) space between each ball. Loosely cover with a cloth, then leave to stand for about 30 minutes, or until doubled in size.

6. Pour the oil into a medium-sized deep saucepan – the oil should be about 5cm (2in) deep – and heat to 160C/325F. Carefully lower 2–3 dough balls at a time into the hot oil and fry each batch for 8 minutes, flipping halfway through, until they are a deep golden brown. Remove with a slotted spoon and drain on kitchen paper. Repeat until all of the doughnuts are cooked. To finish, roll the warm fried doughnuts in the caster sugar.

7. Once cool, use the end of a dessert spoon to make a hole in one side of each doughnut. Wiggle the handle around to create a space for the custard. Spoon the custard into a piping bag fitted with a 0.5mm (¼in) round nozzle and fill the doughnuts with custard. Serve immediately.

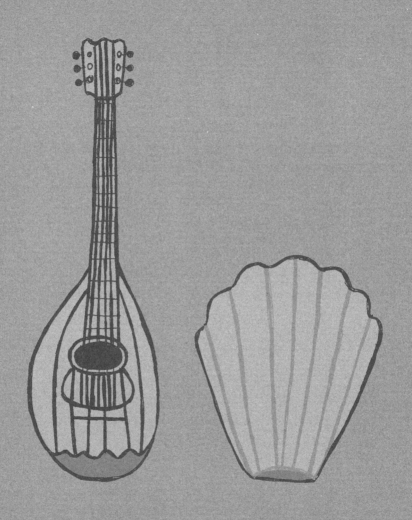

CAPTAIN CORELLI'S MADELEINES

CLASSIC FRENCH MADELEINES

~~~~~~

They do say you should beware Greek islanders bearing gifts, but if they taste as good as these buttery bakes, an exception must be made. Here, the madeleines' unique shell shape is magically transmuted to the musical form of Captain Corelli's mandolin. Love is what is left when the passion has gone – or when the last crumbs of these meltingly moreish bites have been devoured …

Makes 12 madeleines

75g/2½oz butter, melted and cooled, plus extra to grease

75g/2½oz self-raising flour, sifted, plus extra to dust

2 eggs, lightly beaten

75g/2½oz caster sugar

zest of 1 lemon

icing sugar, to dust

1. Heat the oven to 220C/425F/gas 7. Brush a 12-hole madeleine tray with melted butter, allow to set for a few seconds then dust with flour, shaking off any excess. Set aside.

2. Whisk the eggs, sugar and lemon zest for 5 minutes, or until pale and doubled in volume. Gently fold in the flour until fully incorporated. Pour the butter around the edge of the bowl and fold in, making sure you keep as much volume as possible. Cover and chill for 45 minutes.

3. Fill each madeleine hole two-thirds full with mixture, then bake for 10–12 minutes or until risen and golden. Allow to cool in the tray for a few minutes then slip the madeleines onto a wire rack to cool completely. Dust with icing sugar before serving.

THE REMAINS OF THE CRÈME BRÛLÉE

CRÈME BRÛLÉE

~~~~~~

T his is, on the whole, an extremely pleasing dessert. The uppermost layer of the crème brûlée is as stiff as the upper lip of Stevens the butler. Its crystallised, hardened surface gleams as brightly as the silverware on the dining table, keeping up appearances with infinite care.

With the passing of time, and perhaps with the wisdom and grace of a friend like Miss Kenton, the hidden depths may reveal themselves to be a softened sort of love, a sweet kind of custard – but perhaps that is an intimacy too far. Best to leave the brûlée unbroken, so that its sugary secrets remain silent and unspoken.

Serves 6

600ml/1 pint double cream
1 vanilla pod, split
4 egg yolks
140g/5oz caster sugar,
plus 1 tbsp

1. Put the cream and vanilla pod into a pan over a low heat and bring slowly to the boil. Remove from the heat, cover and set aside for at least 30 minutes to infuse. Set six ovenproof ramekins in a roasting tin.

2. Heat oven to 150C/300F/gas 2. Beat the egg yolks with the tablespoon of caster sugar. Strain in the vanilla cream and stir to combine, then pour into the ramekins.

3. Pour hand-hot water into the roasting dish to come halfway up the sides of the ramekins, then cook in the oven for 30–35 minutes or until just set but with a slight wobble. Remove from the oven and allow to cool. Take out of the roasting tin, cover, and chill overnight.

4. The next day, put the ramekins on a baking sheet and sprinkle the remaining sugar over the top of them in an even layer. Heat the grill to hot, or use a blowtorch to brûlée the tops – the sugar will be beginning to bubble and turning a rich golden brown. Set aside in a cool place – but not the fridge – for up to an hour before serving.

TART OF DARKNESS

DARK CHOCOLATE AND CARAMEL TART

~~~~~

A tale of the dark continent requires a Tart of Darkness. Set sail on the waterways of the Congo for a confectionery masterclass like no other. Rivers of caramel combine with wickedly dark Belgian chocolate, all finished with a flourish of ivory cream. You don't have to be feeling (Mar)low to appreciate this African eye-opener. Kurtz into the tart with a super-sharp knife and share the heavenly taste alongside 'the horror, the horror …'

Serves 8

375g block ready-made shortcrust pastry

5 tbsp ready-made thick caramel sauce

3 tbsp crunchy peanut butter

200g/7oz Belgian plain chocolate, roughly chopped

knob of butter

200ml/7fl oz double cream

handful salted peanuts, roughly chopped

1. Heat the oven to 190C/375F/gas 5. Roll out the pastry and use to line a 23cm (9in) fluted tart tin. Trim off any excess pastry, then chill for 30 minutes.

2. Put the tart tin on a baking sheet, scrunch up a large piece of baking paper and place it inside the pastry case, and fill it with baking beans. Bake for 15 minutes, remove from the oven, lift out the baking paper and beans, then return to the oven to cook for a further 10 minutes, or until golden. Leave to cool.

3. Spread the tart base with the caramel sauce then swirl through the peanut butter. Chill for 20 minutes.

4. To make the chocolate filling, put the chocolate in a heatproof bowl with the butter. Heat the double cream to just boiling point, remove from the heat and pour over the chocolate. Allow to stand for 5 minutes, then stir until smooth. Spoon this over the caramel and peanut butter, smooth the top and scatter with chopped salted peanuts. Chill for 2 hours or until ready to serve.

WAR & A PIECE ...
OF CHEESECAKE

WHITE RUSSIAN CHEESECAKE

~~~

Tolstoy's novel is renowned as one of the longest in history; happily, this dish is a cakewalk in the park to make – it'll be done before you can say, 'Princess Anna Mikhaylovna Drubetskaya'. Introducing the flavours of the famous White Russian cocktail, this is a cheesecake that boasts a culinary complexity to rival the sprawling storylines of the book. *Bon appétit*, as the French-speaking Russian aristocrats would say ...

Serves 8–10

140g/5oz butter, melted, plus extra for greasing
250g/9oz digestive biscuits
1 tsp ground cinnamon

For the filling
600g/1lb 5oz full-fat cream cheese
200g/7oz soft light brown sugar
3 whole eggs, plus 1 yolk
150ml/¼ pint sour cream
1 tsp vanilla extract
zest of 1 lemon

For the topping
50ml/2½fl oz coffee-flavoured liqueur
50ml/2½fl oz vodka
50g/2oz caster sugar
50g/2oz raisins

1. Grease and line the base and sides of a 20cm (8in) round springform cake tin with baking paper. Whizz the biscuits in a food processor, or crush them with a rolling pin, to fine crumbs. Add the melted butter and cinnamon and stir to combine. Press the buttery crumbs into the prepared tin and chill for about 1 hour or until firm.

2. Heat the oven to 180C/350F/gas 4. Using an electric mixer, beat the cream cheese until smooth. Beat in the sugar, then gradually add the eggs and egg yolk, sour cream, vanilla extract and lemon zest. Scrape the mixture onto the base and smooth the surface with back of a spoon. Cover the outside and base of the tin with a layer of foil, and place it in a large roasting tin. Pour boiling water around the tin so that it comes about halfway up the side. Cook for about 50 minutes – the cheesecake should feel set, but with a bit of a wobble. Remove from the oven and allow to cool, then chill overnight.

3. Meanwhile, make the White Russian raisin topping. Put all the ingredients in a saucepan and simmer until the syrup has reduced a little. Allow to cool and chill in the fridge overnight. Serve the cheesecake with the raisin syrup drizzled over the top.

CATCH-TIRAMISU

CLASSIC TIRAMISU

~~~~~~

I t was love at first sight: the Italian pudding and the Italian-based World War Two fighter pilot. Comrades in arms.

For Yossarian, there was only one cache and that was the cache of tiramisu hidden in his gun turret on the plane. Yossarian wanted to eat it, yet wanting to eat such a delicious coffee-flavoured concoction clearly proved he was sane. It was a mind(erbinder)-bending dilemma.

Only one thing was certain. It was a major, major, major, majorly tasty treat.

Serves 6–8

2 x 500g tubs mascarpone cheese
50g/2oz caster sugar
3 eggs, separated
250ml/9fl oz coffee liqueur
425ml/14fl oz strong cold black coffee
30 Italian sponge fingers
cocoa powder, to dust

1. Put the mascarpone, sugar and egg yolks in a bowl and beat until creamy. In another clean bowl, beat the egg whites to stiff peaks. Fold one-third of the whites into the mascarpone to loosen, then fold in the rest and fully combine. Spoon a quarter of this mixture into the base of a 20 x 20cm (8 x 8in) rectangular serving dish.

2. Mix the coffee liqueur and cold coffee together in a small bowl, then dip the sponge fingers into the liquid one at a time, turning to coat. Lay a single layer of soaked sponge fingers on top of the mascarpone mix. Top with another quarter of the remaining mascarpone and another layer of sponge fingers.

3. Continue until all of the sponge fingers are used up, finishing with a layer of mascarpone. Smooth the top and sprinkle liberally with cocoa powder. Cover and chill for 24 hours. Serve chilled.

LES MISÉR-MARBLE CAKE

MARBLED RING CAKE WITH LEMON GLAZE AND EDIBLE FLOWERS

~~~~~

D o you hear the people sing? They're chorusing for the two great exports of the nineteenth century: mouthwatering marble cake from Germany and Victor Hugo's celebrated historical novel, *Les Misérables*, from France. This is a story – and a cake – of contrasts. Jean Valjean versus Javert, Eponine versus Cosette in the battle for Marius's heart, and the vibrant yellow lemon versus the delicate rose-pink. They swirl together in an unstoppable chain of events that will have show-stopping consequences. Barricade the doors and tuck in. Revolutionary!

Serves 8

140g/5oz unsalted butter, plus extra for greasing

250g/9oz plain flour, plus extra for dusting

1½ tsp baking powder

½ tsp bicarbonate of soda

200g/7oz caster sugar

3 eggs, lightly beaten

200ml/7fl oz buttermilk

1 tsp vanilla extract

zest of 1 lemon, plus juice of ½

1 tsp rosewater

a few drops of pink food colouring

1. Heat the oven to 180C/375F/gas 4. Grease and flour a ring tin which is 25cm (10in) diameter and 5cm (2in) deep. Put the flour, baking powder and bicarbonate of soda into a bowl and mix. In a separate bowl, beat the butter and sugar with an electric whisk until pale and fluffy. Gradually add the eggs, alternating with a tablespoon of the flour mixture, then gently fold in the rest of the flour. Stir in the buttermilk and vanilla.

2. Remove two-thirds of the batter and mix in the lemon zest and juice. Add the rosewater and pink food colouring to the remaining batter. Pour the lemon batter into the prepared cake tin and spread it out evenly. Spoon the rose batter on top, then smooth it down and swirl it through with a skewer or knife to create a marbled effect.

For the icing

2 tbsp lemon juice

200g/7oz icing sugar, sifted

selection of edible flower
or crystallised flowers, to
decorate

3. Bake for about 25 minutes, until well risen and firm to the
touch. Remove from the oven, transfer to a wire rack and leave
to cool completely.

4. Meanwhile, make the icing. Whisk the lemon juice into
the icing sugar, adding a splash of cold water until you have
a smooth, runny icing. Drizzle the icing over the cake then
decorate with the flowers of your choice.

TO KILL A BATTENBERG

CHOCOLATE AND ALMOND BATTENBERG CAKE

〜〜〜

The black-and-white checkerboard of this chocolate-and-almond Battenberg bake sets the scene for a dangerous game: an unforgettable tale in which white or black can mean life or death – and justice threatens to be as malleable as marzipan. I won't Harp(er) on about it, but you could Scout around and still not find a more scrumptious slice of the Deep South. And that's the Boo-tiful truth.

Serves 8–10

250g/9oz soft butter, plus extra for greasing

250g/9oz caster sugar

200g/9oz self-raising flour

50g/2oz ground almonds

½ tsp almond extract

3 eggs, lightly beaten

100ml/4fl oz fat-free natural yogurt

2 tbsp cocoa powder

splash of milk

1. Heat oven to 180C/350F/gas 4. Make a barrier down the centre of a 20 x 30cm (8 x 12in) tin with a double layer of foil, using a little butter to hold it in place. Grease and line each half with baking paper.

2. Put all the cake ingredients except the cocoa powder into a large mixing bowl and beat until smooth. Put half of the mixture into one side of the tin and smooth the surface. Fold the cocoa into the remaining mixture, adding a splash of milk if it seems dry. Tip the chocolate mix into the other side of the tin, smooth the surface and bake for 50–55 minutes, or until a skewer inserted into the centre comes out clean. Allow to cool completely in the tin. Carefully tip out onto a chopping board.

3. Place the cakes side by side and trim both ends to make sure they are the same length. You may need to run a bread knife over the surface to ensure the cakes are level. Brush off any crumbs, then split each half in 2 along their length so that you have two white and two chocolate long rectangular sponges.

For the decoration
200g/7oz chocolate spread
icing sugar, to dust
500g pack white marzipan

4. Spoon the chocolate spread into a bowl and heat for a few seconds in the microwave to loosen. To assemble the Battenberg, lightly dust the work surface with icing sugar. Roll out the marzipan to approximately 45 x 35cm (18 x 14in). Spread a couple of tablespoons of chocolate spread over the surface. Lay one white and one chocolate cake down the centre of the marzipan. Spread the middle and all sides with chocolate spread then push them together so they are snug. Place the remaining two sponges on top in a chequerboard pattern, coating their sides and middle with chocolate spread.

5. Fold the marzipan over the cakes and press the edges together. Smooth the surface with your hands then carefully flip the cake over, seam-side down, and place on a serving plate. Trim both ends to neaten and reveal your chocolate and almond Battenberg sponges.

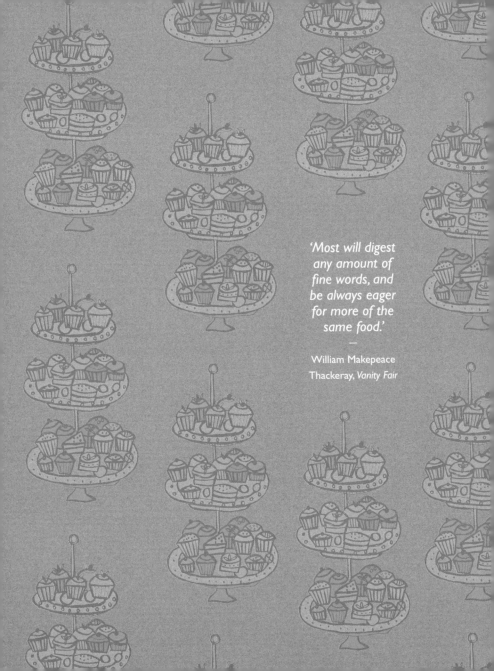

'Most will digest
any amount of
fine words, and
be always eager
for more of the
same food.'
—

William Makepeace
Thackeray, *Vanity Fair*

TRAGEDY
& DRAMA

ONE FLEW OVER THE COOKIES' NEST

FRUIT AND NUT COOKIES

The Chief thing to say about these fruit-and-nut cookies is that they are maddeningly good. Let Randle McMurphy lead you into rebellion and temptation till you're nursing a cookie overdose. There's nothing unto-ward about them. Help yourself to a Billy Bibbit or two, but whatever you do: Don't tell Ratched.

Makes 30 cookies

100g/4oz soft butter

140g/5oz caster sugar

1 egg, lightly beaten

140g/5oz self-raising flour

100g/4oz crunchy peanut butter

100g/4oz raisins

50g/2oz salted peanuts, roughly chopped

1. Heat the oven to 190C/375F/gas 5. Line a couple of baking trays with baking paper. Put all the ingredients except the raisins and peanuts in a bowl and beat until smooth. Stir in the raisins and peanuts.

2. Spoon heaped teaspoons of the cookie mixture onto the baking trays, leaving room between each for the cookies to spread. Bake for 12–15 minutes, or until the cookies are golden brown around the edges. Allow to cool slightly on the tray then transfer to a wire rack to cool completely.

MRS DALLOWAFERS

CINNAMON AND HONEY WAFERS WITH RASPBERRIES

M rs Dalloway said that she would make the wafers herself. She tossed the ingredients into the bowl with the same gay abandon which she had used to greet Sally Seton at Bourton. What an absolute jaunt! The pure gilt of the honey as it dripped thickly from her spoon recalled to mind the interminable slog of married life. Perhaps instead she should have opted for the light dusting of the Indian spice of cinnamon. She decided she would have both, bundled up and baked into a round of perfect wafer, and invited along to the party tonight. She meshed the past and present, wafer and filling, into one creative canapé, and dotted them with the raspberries of revolution, the pursuit of happiness, the self-immolation of Septimus. She hoped it would be a night to remember.

Makes 8 wafers

50g/2oz butter at room temperature

75g/2½oz icing sugar, plus extra to dust

4 tbsp runny honey

I egg white, lightly beaten

75g/2½oz plain flour

I tsp ground cinnamon

For the filling

300ml/½ pint double cream

150ml/¼ pint Greek yoghurt

I tbsp icing sugar, plus extra to dust

2 tbsp framboise or kirsch (optional)

350–450g/12–14oz raspberries

1. Heat the oven to 200C/400F/gas 6. Line a couple of baking trays with baking paper. Beat the butter, icing sugar and honey until pale and creamy, stir in the egg white, then add the flour and cinnamon and combine to make a smooth batter.

2. Drop 4–6 heaped teaspoonfuls of the mixture onto each baking tray, spacing them well apart, and spread out to 7.5cm (3in) rounds using the back of a spoon. Bake in the oven for 5–7 minutes until golden. Carefully lift off the baking tray with a palette knife and transfer to a wire rack to cool and crisp. Continue baking until you have used up all of the mixture – you should make about 24 wafers.

3. To make the filling, whip the cream to soft peaks. Fold in the yoghurt, sugar and liqueur, if using. To assemble, layer up the wafers in threes, sandwiching them together with the cream and a few raspberries. Dust generously with icing sugar and serve immediately.

MIDDLEMARSH-MALLOWS

PEPPERMINT MARSHMALLOWS

~~~~~~~~

T his heavily populated serving tray – thriving with the stories and secrets of a multitude of marshmallows – encapsulates the essence of the bustling town of Middlemarch itself. With no central hero or centrepiece as such, this dish succeeds thanks to its wide-ranging assortment of peppermint-flavoured fancies. The soft and spongy sweets have a surprising density; layer after layer is revealed with each and every mouthful. By George (Eliot), they're good.

Makes about 36 small squares

50g/2oz icing sugar
50g/2oz cornflour
10 gelatine sheets
500g/1lb 2oz caster sugar
1 tbsp glucose syrup
2 egg whites
2 tsp peppermint essence
mint-green food colouring

1. Combine the icing sugar and cornflour. Lightly grease a 20 x 30cm (8 x 12in) baking tin and dust it with most of the icing sugar and cornflour mix.

2. Melt the gelatine leaves in 150ml (¼ pint) hot water and keep warm.

3. In a large pan, stir the sugar, glucose and 200ml (7fl oz) of water over a low heat until the sugar dissolves, then bring to a boil until the mixture reaches 125C/256F or firm ball stage on a sugar thermometer. If you don't have a thermometer, drop a little mixture into very cold water – the ball should stretch between your fingers into pliable strands. Pour the melted gelatine into the sugar syrup – it will bubble up, so stand back.

4. Meanwhile, beat the egg whites with an electric whisk in a large clean bowl to stiff peaks. Gradually add the boiling sugar syrup, whisking, with the peppermint essence and food colouring. Beat for 8–10 minutes until very firm and glossy.

5. Tip the mix into the tin, smooth the top, then dust with the remaining icing sugar and cornflour. Set aside in a cool place until firm – but not the fridge. Turn out and cut into squares.

ETON MESS OF THE D'URBERVILLES

ETON MESS

~~~~~~~

The pure white innocence of the milkmaid's double cream is here whipped up into the soft peaks of a devastating dish. The meringues of her dreams are crushed up and scattered, and all is seasoned with the irresistible burgundy berries of the dangerous D'Urbervilles. Ah, those juicy mouthfuls of sinful strawberries, be-ribboning the guiltless cream with shards of ruby red. One simply longs for an Angelic finale to this epic Eton Mess.

Serves 12–15

4 egg whites
25g/1oz caster sugar
200g/7oz soft light brown sugar
200g/7oz strawberries, hulled and chopped
200g/7oz raspberries
juice of 1 lemon
1 tbsp icing sugar
400ml/14fl oz double cream

1. Heat the oven to 140C/275F/gas 1. Line a couple of baking sheets with non-stick baking paper.

2. To make the meringue, whisk the egg whites to stiff peaks. Gradually whisk in the caster sugar and the brown sugar, whisking between each addition to dissolve the sugar until you have very stiff, glossy meringues.

3. Spoon heaped tablespoons of the meringue onto the lined baking sheets. Bake for 1 hour, or until puffed, lightly golden and firm. Leave them in the oven with the door slightly open to allow to cool completely.

4. Put the berries in a large bowl with the lemon juice and icing sugar and allow to stand for 5 minutes, or until the fruits start to release some of their juices. Whip the cream to soft peaks then fold through the juicy berries to create a ripple effect.

5. To serve, lightly crush the meringues into the cream mixture so you have some small and some larger chewy meringue pieces. Spoon into serving glasses and serve.

THE COLOR PROFITEROLES

PURPLE PROFITEROLES WITH WHITE CHOCOLATE ICING

~~~

Dear God,

These here profiteroles are just about the most beautiful desserts I ever saw. They 'bout hundred thousand times more beautiful than something you might see in a white person's cookbook. They drippin' in chocolate and stuffed full of fresh cream and berries and overflowin' with rivers of cassis. And the color! Oh Lord, that color. The color purple. I just want you to know, God – you little old white man, or whoever you are – I've noticed it. I did not walk by without registerin' that color purple. In a field or on a plate – it's just beautiful. For me, these here profiteroles are Shug in her fur coats, they're the sun shining in the yard, they are my children, they are my independence – they are all the good things in life. And they taste damn sweet.

Serves 6–8

85g/3oz butter, diced
140g/5oz plain flour, sifted
3 eggs, lightly beaten

For the filling
200g/7oz mixed fruit
(such as blackberries
and blackcurrants),
roughly chopped
3 tbsp cassis

1. Heat the oven to 200C/400F/gas 6. Line a couple of baking trays with baking paper. Put the butter into a medium-sized pan with 225ml (8fl oz) water and heat gently to melt. Once the butter has melted, increase the heat and bring to the boil. Remove from the heat, add the sifted flour and beat the mixture with a wooden spoon until you get a smooth, shiny dough that leaves the sides of the pan. Tip into a mixing bowl and allow to cool for 5 minutes.

2. Gradually add the eggs and continue to beat until you have a smooth dough that falls reluctantly from the spoon. Dollop tablespoon-sized balls of mixture onto the prepared baking trays, leaving space between them to puff up. Bake for

2 tbsp icing sugar, plus extra
for dusting

300ml/½ pint double cream

To finish

150g/4¼oz white chocolate,
chopped

a little purple food colouring

25 minutes, until golden and crisp. Remove from the oven
and poke a hole in the bottom of each. Place the profiteroles
hole side up on the baking trays and return to the oven for
5 minutes to dry out and crisp up further. Remove from the
oven, transfer to a wire rack and allow to cool completely.

3. To make the filling, put the fruit in a bowl with 2 tablespoons
of cassis and a tablespoon of icing sugar, stir, and allow to stand
for 5 minutes. Meanwhile, put the cream into a large mixing
bowl with the remaining icing sugar and whip it to soft peaks.
Gently fold the berries and any juices through the cream. Use a
couple of teaspoons to fill the profiteroles with the purple-
fruit and cream mix.

4. Put the white chocolate in a heatproof bowl with the
remaining tablespoon of cassis and purple food colouring, set
over a pan of barely simmering water and stir until melted.
Remove from the heat allow to cool for a few minutes then
spoon over the filled profiteroles. Enjoy.

BANANA KARENINA

TOFFEE TRUFFLE BOMBES
WITH CARAMELISED BANANAS

~~~~~~

Happy families are all alike; every unhappy family is unhappy in its own way. But happy or sad, these toffee truffle bombes will be a hit for family suppers every time. Decadently decorated to mirror the beautiful ballgowns of Anna and Kitty, they're as tasty as a fresh-faced debutante daring to dream of love, and as rich as a Russian aristocrat. The side order of bananas summons the sexuality of Vronsky himself, drizzled with the caramel of infidelity and laced with illicit desire. Watch you don't go off the rails …

Serves 6

For the toffee ice cream
150g (5oz) toffees
150ml/¼ pint milk
150ml/¼ pint double cream
75g/3oz fromage frais oil, for greasing

For the chocolate ganache
150ml/¼ pint double cream
140g/5oz plain chocolate, in small pieces

1. To make the toffee ice cream, place the toffees in the freezer for 30 minutes, then cut them into small chunks. Set aside 50g/2oz of chopped toffees. Melt the rest with the milk in a saucepan over a low heat, stirring occasionally, until smooth. Remove from the heat and allow to cool completely.

2. Whip the cream in a bowl until you have soft, floppy peaks, then stir in the fromage frais and the cooled toffee mixture. Spoon into a shallow freezerproof container, cover and freeze for 3–4 hours until firm.

3. Lightly oil six 120ml/4fl oz individual metal pudding basins or freezerproof cups, line them with cling film, then put in the freezer to chill. Turn the ice cream into a bowl and beat well with a wooden spoon, then divide between the pudding moulds. Spread it evenly up the sides of each mould, leaving a hollow in the centre. Freeze for 30 minutes until firm.

For the caramelised bananas

4 hard bananas, peeled and sliced into 1cm/¼ in pieces

50g/2oz soft light brown sugar

50ml/2fl oz double cream

4. To make the ganache, place the cream in a saucepan and bring almost to the boil. Remove from the heat, add the chocolate and leave undisturbed for 5 minutes. Stir to a smooth cream, then chill until thickened. Beat lightly, then spoon into the centre of the toffee bombes and level the tops. Freeze until firm.

5. Meanwhile, make the caramel bananas. Fry the bananas in a large non-stick frying pan for a few minutes on each side until turning golden. Add the sugar and double cream and swirl the pan to melt the sugar, then increase the heat and allow to bubble for 1 minute. Remove from the heat.

6. To serve, turn out the bombes onto cold plates and peel off the cling film. Scatter the reserved toffee chunks on top, divide the caramel bananas between the plates and drizzle over any caramel sauce.

FINNEGANS CAKE

CHOCOLATE AND GUINNESS CAKE

Riverrun of freshly flowing Guinness makes this Finnegans Cake a tasty treat to delight the soul and senses, a joy for Joyce we jeer, and a peck of plain flour butter sugar stout bicarbonate and the baking soda, not forgetting eggs and cocoa magic powder, we mix it all up and stir and stir, the Dublin Liffey itself could not be thicker or more life-giving than this pure beauty of a mixing bowl bazaar and so after the bake must come the icing what do we need but a lone a last a loved a

Serves 8

100g/4oz soft butter, plus extra for greasing
280g/10oz soft light brown sugar
200ml/7fl oz stout
50g/2oz cocoa powder
2 eggs, lightly beaten
175g/6oz plain flour
¼ tsp baking powder
1 tsp bicarbonate of soda

For the icing
100g/4oz icing sugar
50g/2oz butter
2 tbsp Guiness or Irish stout
100g/4oz dark chocolate, melted and cooled

1. Heat the oven to 180C/350F/gas 4. Grease and line the base of two 20cm (8in) cake tins. Cream the butter and sugar together until smooth and fluffy, then stir in the stout, cocoa powder and eggs. In another bowl, combine the flour, baking powder and bicarbonate of soda, then fold this into the wet ingredients and stir until combined.

2. Divide the mixture between the cake tins and cook for 30 minutes, or until the cakes are springy to the touch and a skewer inserted into the centre comes out clean. Remove from the oven and allow to cool for a few minutes in the tin, then transfer to a wire rack and leave to cool completely.

3. To make the icing, beat the icing sugar, butter and stout together then stir in the cooled melted chocolate. Spread half of the icing over the top of one cake, sandwich with the other cake then spread the remaining icing over. Chill until ready to serve.

BOOK CLUB EVENING

Something for everyone – a cake, a bake, a biscuit to suit any book you may be reading. Let people guess which book you will be reading next by the bake you have made. This yummy threesome shouldn't be too difficult a starting point for a game of 'guess the book title'.

~~~

ON THE ROCKY ROAD

American Rocky Road (see page 90)

—

RABBIT, RUM BABA

Rum babas (see page 96)

—

ETON MESS OF THE D'URBERVILLES

Eton mess (see page 76)

~~~

Serve with a good book and plenty of wine.

THE GRAPEFRUIT GATSBY

PINK GRAPEFRUIT AND GIN SORBET WITH PROSECCO FIZZ

~~~~~

T he Roaring Twenties. The Great Jazz Age. Be borne back ceaselessly into the past with this decadent cocktail of bootlegged gin liquor and pink, pink grapefruit sorbet. It always looks so cool …

Jay Gatsby himself would surely approve, so Daisy, Daisy, give me your answer do: one scoop or two?

Top it all off with Prosecco and get (Nick) carried away with the exorbitant glitz and glamour of The Grapefruit Gatsby.

Serves 4–6

juice and zest of 8 pink grapefruit
200g/7oz caster sugar
140ml/5fl oz water
50ml/2fl oz gin
2 tbsp orange flower water
1 egg white
1 bottle Prosecco, chilled

1. Put the grapefruit zest and juice into a pan with the sugar and water. Heat gently to dissolve the sugar, then increase the heat and boil for 3 minutes. Remove from the heat and allow to cool completely.

2. Stir the gin and orange flower water into the sugar syrup, then strain it into a bowl. In another, clean, bowl, beat the egg white until just frothy, then whisk into the orange mixture. For optimum results, freeze in an ice-cream maker, or pour into a shallow freezerproof container and freeze until the sorbet is almost frozen, about 3–4 hours, then mash well with a fork and refreeze until solid.

3. Transfer the sorbet to the fridge for 30 minutes before serving to soften slightly. To serve the Gatsby way, scoop a ball of sorbet into the bottom of a champagne flute and top up with Prosecco.

'I never saw anyone enjoy a pudding so much, I think; and he laughed, when it was all gone, as if his enjoyment of it lasted still.'

—

Charles Dickens,
David Copperfield

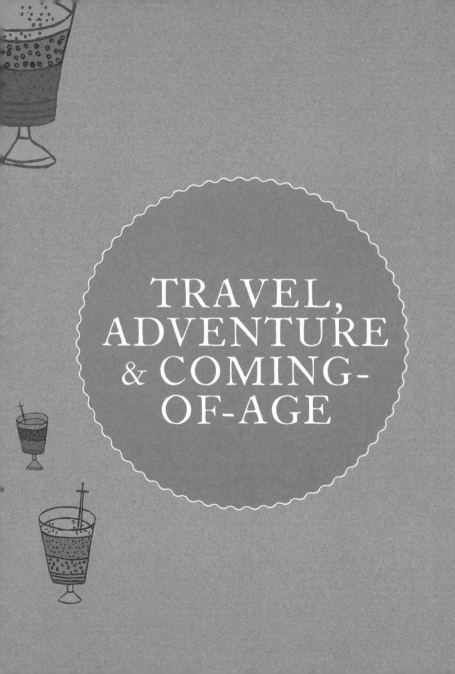

TRAVEL, ADVENTURE & COMING-OF-AGE

DON BISCOTTI

FRUITY, NUTTY AND CHOCOLATY BISCOTTI

H ola! Prepare for a Spanish adventure like no other. Take leave of your senses and your ordinary life – and prepare to go anything but gently into that good knight. Combine nuts, cherries and chocolate chips with a chivalric code of honour, consume a dangerous amount of literature, and then unsheathe your sausage-shaped sword of glory: the Don Biscotti. Thou hast seen nothing yet.

Makes 50 biscotti

100g/4oz caster sugar

50g/2oz softened butter

2 eggs, lightly beaten

1 tsp vanilla extract

250g/9oz plain flour, plus extra for dusting

½ tsp bicarbonate of soda

50g/2oz pistachios, roughly chopped

50g/2oz almonds, roughly chopped

85g/3oz dried sour cherries, roughly chopped

50g/2oz dark chocolate chips

1. Heat the oven to 180C/350F/gas 4. Line a couple of baking trays with baking paper. Beat the sugar and butter until combined. Gradually add the eggs and vanilla extract and beat until light and fluffy. In another bowl mix the flour, bicarbonate of soda, nuts, cherries and chocolate chips. Stir the dry ingredients into the egg mixture to form a soft dough.

2. Knead the dough briefly on a lightly floured surface – it will be quite sticky. Halve the dough and with damp hands shape each half into a 25cm (10in) sausage shape. Lay on the prepared baking tray, flatten slightly, then bake for 25–30 minutes or until lightly browned and firm. Remove from the oven and allow to cool for 10 minutes.

3. Reduce the oven to 160C/325F/gas 3. Use a serrated knife to cut the logs into 1cm (½in) thick diagonal slices. Place on the baking trays cut-sides up. Bake for 15 minutes, turning halfway through, until crisp and golden. Remove from the oven and transfer to a wire rack to cool. Serve with sweet wine, coffee or ice cream.

GREAT ECCLES-SPECTATIONS

ECCLES CAKES

These traditional Eccles cakes would be well worth escaping prison for, even with an iron on your leg. It's enough to make you terrorise small boys for a taste of freedom. So make like a (Mag)witch and cast a spell on soft light sugar, currants and mixed peel. Throw away the lemon Pips but use the zest of life to see the error of your ways, and let's be Havisham of these tasty cakes. Best served at twenty to nine.

Makes 20 Eccles cakes

500g block ready-made puff pastry
flour, for dusting

For the filling
200g/7oz currants
75g/2½oz soft light brown sugar
50g/2oz mixed peel, finely chopped
zest of 2 lemons

To finish
1 egg white, lightly beaten
granulated sugar, to sprinkle
75g/2½oz butter, melted

1. Heat the oven to 220C/425F/gas 7. Line a couple of baking trays with baking paper. Mix all of the filling ingredients together then set aside.

2. Roll out half the pastry on a lightly floured work surface to a roughly 50 x 20cm (20 x 8in) rectangle. Cut in half lengthwise then cut each strip into 5 equal pieces. Do the same with the remaining pastry.

3. Divide the filling between the pastry rectangles, putting a dollop in the centre. Bring the four corners and the edges together, pinching to seal, flip over and lay seam side down on the baking trays. Flatten slightly with your hand then use a sharp knife to slash each Eccles cake on top a couple of times. Brush with a little beaten egg white and sprinkle with sugar. Bake for 12–15 minutes, or until puffed up and golden.

4. Remove from the oven and allow to cool for a few minutes, then pour a drop of butter into each Eccles cake and eat while still warm.

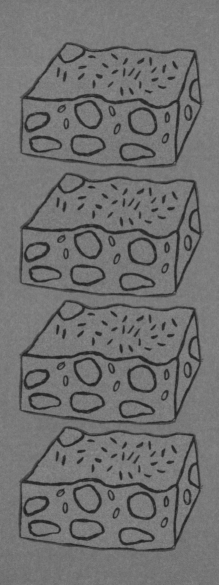

ON THE ROCKY ROAD

AMERICAN ROCKY ROAD

~~~~~

T his Rocky Road is a little slice of (Sal) Paradise. It could almost drive you crazy with its tempting mix of marshmallows, peanuts, cookies, thick chocolate and the open road. Jazz it all up with a sprinkling of icing sugar, if you like, or you could wait not a Beat (Generation) longer, and tuck in for a taste of America that will blow your mind.

Makes 20 squares

250g/9oz chocolate chip cookies

25g/1oz puffed rice cereal

50g/2oz sultanas

50g/2oz salted peanuts

75g/2½oz mini marshmallows

300g/11oz plain chocolate, roughly chopped

100g/4oz butter, diced

100g/4oz golden syrup

1. Line a 20 x 20cm tin with baking parchment. Put the biscuits in a large bowl and use the end of a rolling pin to gently crush them to get a mixture of big chunks and small crumbs. Mix the biscuits with the puffed rice, sultanas, nuts and mini marshmallows, then set aside.

2. Melt the chocolate, butter and golden syrup in a bowl set over a pan of simmering water, stirring occasionally, until smooth. Pour this melted mixture over the crushed biscuit mix and stir together until everything is combined.

3. Tip into the prepared tin and flatten the top lightly, then chill for 2–3 hours or overnight. When set, cut into 20 small squares.

AFTERNOON TEA

Dust off your tea cups and polish your cake forks – it's time for tea.

~~~~~~

SCONE WITH THE WIND

Classic scone with Scarlett O'Hara strawberry jam (see page 12)

—

THE HOBBISCUIT

Pistachio biscuits (see page 126)

—

LORD OF THE MILLEFEUILLES

Strawberries and cream millefeuilles (see page 110)

~~~~~~

Serve with finger sandwiches, tea and Champagne.

SHORTBREAD REVISITED

CLASSIC SHORTBREAD

I n the (March)main, this delectable shortbread is hard to top. It's not a Flyte of fancy to describe it as the English nobility of nosh. Its crisp architectural lines would stun even an impressionable undergraduate. Sweet and buttery, it's the perfect fare for a teddy bears' picnic hosted by Aloysius. In the name of the Father, the Son and the Holy Spirit of period dramas, Amen.

Makes 18 biscuits

225g/8oz soft butter
140g/5oz caster sugar
225g/8oz plain flour, plus extra for dusting
140g/4oz rice flour
caster sugar, for sprinkling

1. Cream the butter and sugar until pale and fluffy. Sift the flours and a pinch of salt into the bowl and cream mix together until the mixture resembles breadcrumbs.

2. Bring the dough together with your hands, tip out on to a lightly floured work surface and knead briefly. Shape the dough into a sausage, about 5cm (2in) thick. Wrap in cling film and chill for an hour or until firm.

3. Heat the oven to 190C/350F/gas 5. Line a couple of baking trays with baking paper. Unwrap the dough, roll in caster sugar, then slice into discs about 1cm thick. Place the biscuits cut side up on the prepared trays and sprinkle over a little more sugar. Bake for 15 minutes, or until pale golden.

4. Allow to cool on the tray for 10 minutes then transfer to a wire rack to cool completely.

THE THREE MOUSSE-KETEERS

MINT CHOCOLATE MOUSSE POTS

T he famous motto begins 'all for one …' and you'll definitely want to keep this mint-choc mousse all to yourself; forget about the 'one for all' bit! As devilishly tasty – and as chilling – as Milady de Winter herself, this mousse is well worth challenging to a duel for. *En garde!*

Serves 6–8

25g/1oz butter

200g/7oz milk chocolate, roughly chopped

100g /4oz plain chocolate, roughly chopped

3 eggs, separated

½ tsp peppermint essence

100ml/3½fl oz double cream

8 crunchy dark chocolate mint sticks, crushed

1. Put the butter, both chocolates, egg yolks, peppermint essence and 1 tablespoon water in a heatproof bowl set over a pan of barely simmering water – do not allow to boil. Stir until you have a smooth velvety mixture. Remove from the heat and allow to cool.

2. Whip the cream to soft peaks. In another bowl, whisk the egg whites until they reach stiff peaks, making sure they do not dry. Fold the whipped cream into the chocolate until fully combined, then using a large metal spoon fold the egg whites in until no visible white remains.

3. Divide the mixture between serving glasses, sprinkle over crushed mint chocolate sticks and chill until required.

RABBIT, RUM BABA

RUM BABAS

$\sim\!\!\sim\!\!\sim$

A re you searching for meaning in a middle-class existence that leaves you strangely dissatisfied? Perhaps you are wondering how you ended up in a dead-end job, in a marriage gone bad? Do you ever get the feeling something's missing from your life?

Well, not any more. These basketball-shaped rum babas are what you've been looking for all along. See how their fluffy sponge shapes fill the gap between your potential and what you have become? Are they not better than a wife, a mistress, a child? Ah, Rabbit, run no more – unless it's straight to the platter to get yourself another serving of these life-affirming wonder balls.

Makes 12 babas

For the babas

100ml/4fl oz milk

25g/1oz butter, plus extra to grease

1 egg, lightly beaten

250g/9oz strong white bread flour, plus extra for dusting

25g/1oz caster sugar

1 x 7g sachet dried fast-action yeast

1. First make the syrup. Put the sugar, cinnamon, vanilla pod and seeds, star anise and 150ml (5fl oz) water into a pan. Slowly bring it to the boil then simmer for 5 minutes, or until slightly reduced and syrupy. Remove from the heat and stir in the rum. Allow to cool.

2. To make the babas, heat the milk to just below boiling point. Remove from the heat, add the butter and swirl the pan to melt it. Leave to cool for about 5 minutes until you can comfortably dip your little finger into the liquid, then stir in the egg.

3. Put the flour, sugar and yeast into a large mixing bowl and stir to combine, then add a pinch of salt. Make a well in the centre of the flour and gradually pour in the milk mixture, stirring, to form a soft, slightly sticky dough.

4. Tip the dough onto a lightly floured work surface and knead for 10 minutes, or until you have a soft, shiny dough. Place the dough into a lightly greased bowl, cover with a clean cloth and leave to stand in a warm spot until doubled in size – about 1 hour.

For the rum syrup

200g/7oz caster sugar

1 cinnamon stick

1 vanilla pod, split and seeds scraped

1 star anise

75ml/2½fl oz dark rum

whipped cream, to serve

5. Tip the dough out onto a floured work surface and knead briefly to get rid of any air bubbles. Flatten the dough slightly and cut into 6 equal parts with a knife, then shape into neat balls. Transfer to two baking trays lined with baking paper, leaving a 5cm (2in) space between each ball. Loosely cover with a cloth and leave to stand for about 30 minutes or until doubled in size.

6. Heat the oven to 180C/350F/gas 4. Bake the doughnuts for about 12–15 minutes, or until the babas are golden and sound hollow when you tap their underside. Transfer to a wire rack to cool.

7. Put the babas into a serving dish, pour over the rum syrup, turning the balls to coat all over, then leave to stand for a few minutes to soak up some of the syrup. Serve with a dollop of whipped cream and any extra syrup poured over the top.

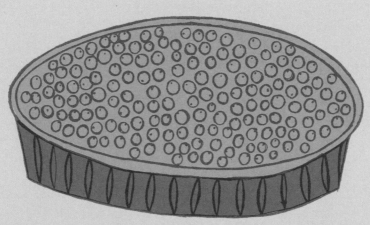

THE ADVENTURES OF HUCKLEBERRY FLAN

BLUEBERRY FLAN

Y ou Mark (Twain) my words: this is a flavoursome flan that will rock your world as well as your boat. First, roll out the pastry and stretch it, like the truth. Make it flat as a life raft. Fill the case with blueberries and cameo roles by Mr Tom Sawyer, as well as the succulent taste of adventure. Take small (Missi) sippis to savour it at its best. It's a pie you'll happily be sold down the river for.

Serves 6–8

375g block shortcrust pastry
3 tbsp blueberry jam
175g/6oz pistachios
2 tbsp plain flour
100g/4oz caster sugar
85g/3oz butter, melted
2 eggs, lightly beaten
140g/5oz blueberries
crème fraîche, to serve

1. Heat the oven to 190C/375F/gas 5. Roll out the pastry to 5mm thickness and use to line a 23cm (9in) round springform cake tin or loose-bottomed tart tin. Trim off any excess pastry and chill for 30 minutes. Scrunch up a piece of baking paper, lay it on top of the pastry and then fill with baking beans. Bake for 10 minutes. Remove from the oven, lift out the baking paper and beans and bake the pastry case, uncovered, for a further 5 minutes, until pale golden. Remove from the oven, cool for a few minutes then spread the blueberry jam over the base.

2. Meanwhile, whizz the pistachios in a food processor with the flour and half of the sugar until finely ground. Tip out into a bowl and add the remaining sugar, melted butter and eggs. Fold through half of the blueberries. Spoon the mixture into the pastry case and smooth the surface. Gently press the remaining blueberries into the surface. Bake for 45–50 minutes, or until the filling is firm to the touch and the pastry is golden.

3. Remove from the oven and cool to room temperature. When cooled, slice and serve with a dollop of crème fraîche.

MOBY SPOTTED DICK

SPOTTED DICK WITH ORANGE SAUCE

~~~~~~~~

C all me Ishmael if this pudding isn't worthy of a naval captain's table. This epic beast of a steamed pud dominates dessert, swimming in a sea of orange-scented sauce. Get your revenge – if you can – by harpooning this hearty dish with knives and silver spoons. Down the hatches with the currant-and-sultana sponge ... for an absolute whale of a time.

Serves 6–8

75g/2½oz soft butter, plus extra for greasing

85g/3oz currants

85g/3oz sultanas

150ml/¼ pint orange juice, plus zest of 1 orange

140g/5oz soft light brown sugar

2 eggs, lightly beaten

175g/6oz self-raising flour, plus 1 tbsp

½ tsp bicarbonate of soda

For the sauce

100g/4oz soft light brown sugar

75g/2½oz butter

100ml/3½fl oz double cream

zest and juice of ½ orange

1. Grease a 1.4 litre (2½ pint) pudding basing and line the base with a circle of baking paper. Put the currants and sultanas in a bowl with the orange juice and zest and leave to stand for about 10 minutes or until the fruit starts to plump up a little.

2. Put the butter, sugar, eggs, flour and bicarbonate of soda into a bowl and beat until smooth. Tip the fruit and orange juice into the mixture and stir to combine – if the mixture looks as though it has curdled, sprinkle over the extra flour and stir again to combine. Scrape into the pudding basin.

3. Cover the basin with a double layer of baking paper and a sheet of foil. Secure with string. Put an upturned saucer into the base of a large pan, sit the pudding basin on top then pour in boiling water from the kettle halfway up the sides of the basin. Cover and steam for 2 hours. Top up with boiling water as necessary during cooking – do not let your pan boil dry.

4. Meanwhile, make the sauce. Heat the sugar, butter, cream and orange zest and juice in a small pan until the sugar dissolves. Boil for 1 minute, then remove from the heat and cool slightly.

5. Remove the pudding from the pan and invert it onto a serving plate. Pour the sauce over, slice it into wedges and serve with any remaining sauce and custard, if you like.

DAVID COFFEE CAKE

RICH COFFEE CAKE

~~~~~

There's no need to be 'umble like the fawning Uriah Heep if you rustle up this classic coffee cake for afternoon tea. Like David himself – who was once described by Dickens as 'his favourite child' – this is a bake that will supplant all others in the sweetness stakes. Cut into it with all the optimism of Mr Micawber and enjoy.

Serves 6–8

100ml/4fl oz sunflower oil, plus extra for greasing

100g/4oz caster sugar

100g/4oz soft light brown sugar

100ml/4fl oz fat-free natural yogurt

200g self-raising flour

2 eggs, lightly beaten

2 tbsp instant coffee power

1 tsp vanilla extract

For the filling

1 tbsp instant coffee powder

4 tbsp coffee liqueur

300ml/½ pint double cream

2 tbsp caster sugar

a handful of chocolate-coated coffee beans, roughly chopped

1. Heat the oven to 190C/350F/gas 5. Grease and line the bases of two 20cm (8in) cake tins with baking paper. Put all of the cake ingredients into a big bowl and beat with an electric whisk until smooth.

2. Divide the cake mixture between the two tins, then bake for 25–30 minutes or until a skewer inserted into the centre comes out clean. Remove the cakes from the oven, allow to cool for a few minutes in their tins then transfer to a wire rack to cool completely.

3. To make the filling, dissolve the coffee powder in 1 tablespoon of boiling water and leave to cool. Prick the cakes all over with a cocktail stick then drizzle 1 tablespoon of the coffee liqueur over each cake. Stir the remaining liqueur into the cooled coffee.

4. Whisk the cream, caster sugar and coffee-liqueur mix to soft peaks. Spread half over one of the cakes, sandwich with the other cake then spread the remaining coffee cream over the top. Scatter with chocolate-coated coffee beans and chill until ready to serve.

THE CATCHER IN THE RYE & HONEY CAKE

PEAR, HONEY AND RYE CAKE

There's nothing phony about this pear, rye and honey cake. Don your best red hunting cap (for this is a cake-eating hat … you eat honey cake in this hat) and simmer resentment along with the elemental ingredients. Cook up a fantasy scenario – whereby you save all the children in the world with this comforting cake – but then Holden your horses and slow down. Everybody feels isolated in New York City, so sit down with a slice and chew the fat with friends and enemies alike.

Serves 6–8

85g/3oz butter, softened, plus extra for greasing

75g/2½oz soft light brown sugar

75g/2½oz runny honey, plus extra to drizzle

1 tsp ground ginger

2 eggs, lightly beaten

100g/4oz rye flour

100g/4oz self-raising flour

1 tsp baking powder

75ml/2½fl oz milk

2 pears, 1 cored and grated, 1 peeled and cut into wedges

vanilla ice cream, to serve

1. Heat the oven to 180C/350F/gas 4. Grease and line a deep 20cm (8in) round springform cake tin with baking paper. Beat the butter, sugar, honey and ginger with electric beaters until pale and creamy. Gradually beat in the eggs. Tip in the flours, baking powder, milk and grated pear and mix until combined.

2. Tip into the prepared tin, dot the pear wedges over the top and bake for 30–35 minutes or until a skewer inserted into the centre comes out clean.

3. Remove from the oven and allow to cool in the tin for 5 minutes, then transfer to a wire rack and brush with extra honey. Serve at room temperature with vanilla ice cream.

'When I've mixed this honey with our breadfruit batter, I'll be ready to serve you a delectable piece of cake.'

—

Jules Verne, *Twenty Thousand Leagues Under the Sea*

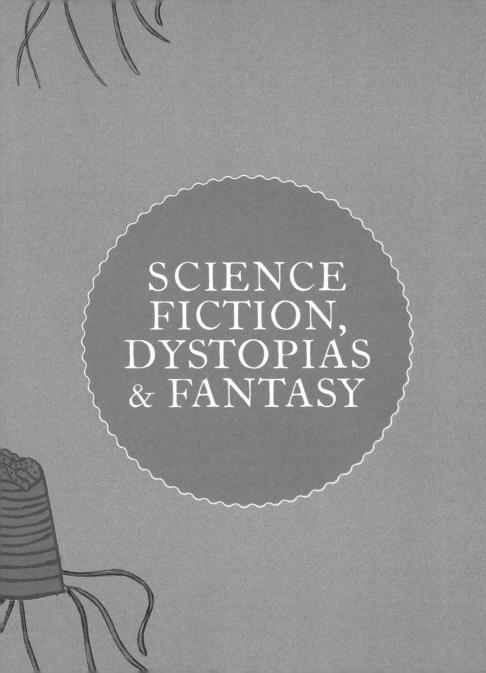

SCIENCE
FICTION,
DYSTOPIAS
& FANTASY

NINETEEN-EIGHTY PETIT FOURS

CHOCOLATE TRUFFLES

~~~~~~~

W hen the clocks are striking thirteen, it's time for tea. Whether in Newspeak, Oldspeak or just plain English, these chocolate truffles are doubleplusgood. Lay out a blanket under the spreading chestnut tree, and indulge in the thoughtcrime of wanting just one, oh one more ...

Makes 20 truffles

140g/5oz plain chocolate, roughly chopped

50g/2oz butter

100g/4oz trifle sponge cakes, crumbled

50g/2oz icing sugar

2 tbsp dark rum, brandy or alcohol of your choice

50g/2oz cocoa powder

1. Put the chocolate and butter in a bowl over a pan of barely simmering water, stir until smooth then stir in the cake crumbs, icing sugar and alcohol of your choice. Stir well, then remove from the heat and chill for 45 minutes or until the mixture is cool enough to handle.

2. Lightly dust your fingers with cocoa and roll the truffle mixture into 20 small balls, roll each truffle in cocoa powder and coat. Arrange the truffles in small fancy cases, then chill until required. Remove from the fridge about 30 minutes before serving.

THE LORD OF THE RING DOUGHNUTS

MARGARITA RING DOUGHNUTS

One ring to rule them all … These sweet, golden doughnuts may cause a war or two as they're simply wizard. Be (Sam)wise and bake a few extra to keep your guests Merry. You might find they become a regular Hobbit. So don't be s-Elvish and keep them to yourself. Present them on a platter to become the best Ring-bearer of them all.

Makes 12 doughnuts

225ml/8fl oz milk
50g/2oz butter, diced
2 eggs, lightly beaten
500g/1lb 2oz strong white bread flour, plus extra for dusting
2 tbsp cocoa powder
50g/2oz caster sugar
1 x 7g sachet dried fast-action yeast

For the topping
200g/9oz icing sugar
edible gold glitter spray
>

1. Heat the milk to just below boiling point. Remove from the heat, add the butter and swirl the pan to melt it. Leave to cool for about 5 minutes or until you can comfortably dip your little finger into the liquid, then stir in the lightly beaten eggs.

2. Put the flour, sugar and yeast into a large mixing bowl and stir to combine, then add a pinch of salt. Make a well in the centre of the flour and gradually pour in the milk mixture, stirring, to form a soft, slightly sticky dough. Tip the dough onto a lightly floured work surface and knead for 10 minutes, or until you have a soft, shiny dough. Place the dough into a lightly greased bowl, cover with a clean cloth and leave to stand in a warm spot until doubled in size – about 1 hour.

3. Tip out the dough onto a floured work surface and knead briefly to get rid of any air bubbles. Flatten the dough to a 2cm (1in) thickness. Use a 7cm (3in) round cutter to stamp out the dough, or cut it into 12 equal parts with a knife, then shape it into neat balls. Plunge the handle of a wooden spoon into the centre of each doughnut, going all the way through to the other side.

>

THE LORD OF THE RING DOUGHNUTS

(cont.)

4. Flip the doughnuts, one at a time, onto the handle and rotate the spoon until the hole is about 6cm (2in) wide. Transfer the doughnuts to two baking trays lined with baking paper, leaving a 5cm (2in) space between each ring. Loosely cover with a cloth and leave to stand for about 30 minutes, or until doubled in size.

5. Heat the oven to 180C/350F/gas 4. Bake the doughnuts for about 12–15 minutes, or until they are golden and sound hollow when you tap their underside. Transfer to a wire rack to cool.

6. For the topping, mix the icing sugar with 2 tablespoons of water in a small bowl set over a pan of barely simmering water. Dip each of the rings into the icing then lay on a wire rack set over a baking tray to set. Once the icing is hard, spray with edible gold glitter spray. Enjoy while still warm.

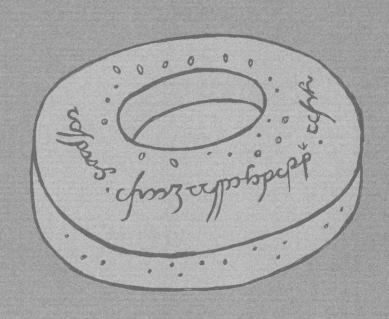

LORD OF THE MILLEFEUILLES

STRAWBERRIES AND CREAM MILLEFEUILLES

I f you were to be stranded on a desert island, these magnificent millefeuilles would be one luxury you'd definitely long for. Savagely good, no rules apply when it comes to combining the puff pastry, sweet jam, cream and strawberries – especially if you don't know Jack about baking. They're a beast of a baked good – a towering stack of sweetness that's enough to turn you into a Piggy. So put your guilty conch-ience to one side and enjoy.

Serves 6

1 x 320g packet ready-rolled puff pastry
75g/2½oz icing sugar

For the filling
300ml/½ pint double cream
1 tbsp icing sugar
1 tsp vanilla extract
100g/4oz strawberries, hulled and sliced
3 tbsp good-quality strawberry jam

1. Heat the oven to 200C/400F/gas 6. Line a large baking tray with baking paper. Unroll the pastry and cut it in half along the length to form two long rectangles. Dust the baking paper with icing sugar and lay the pastry on top, leaving a gap between the two rectangles. Dust the top with more icing sugar and rub it into the pastry to coat. Lightly prick the pastry all over with a fork then cover with a piece of baking paper and place a flat baking tray on top. Weigh down the tray with a large ovenproof dish and bake for 25 minutes.

2. Remove from the oven, take off the dish, baking tray and paper and the pastry should be golden and crisp. If it isn't, return it to the oven and cook for a further 5 minutes. Once done, remove from the oven and cool completely.

3. To make the filling, whip the cream, icing sugar and vanilla extract to soft peaks. Put a slice of pastry onto a serving plate or chopping board, spread with the cream then arrange the strawberries on top. Spread the jam on the other piece of pastry and put it jam side down on top of the strawberries. Dust the top heavily with icing sugar and cut into generous slices.

A CHOC-WORK ORANGE

CHOCOLATE AND ORANGE JAFFA CUPCAKES

W hat's it going to be then, eh? Gather round, my little droogies, get your otchkies out and feast your glazzies. What do you viddy? Only some horrorshow sladky pishcha. Don't creech! They're bolshy ones. There's enough for all our zoobies to bite into. No dratsing. Wash them down with a cold glass of moloko. Ahh ... Choodessny.

Makes 6 cupcakes

100g/4oz self-raising flour

75g/2½oz soft light brown sugar

1 egg, lightly beaten

2 tbsp sunflower oil, plus extra for greasing

100g/4oz fat-free natural yoghurt

zest of 1 orange

For the topping

85g/3oz plain chocolate flavoured with orange (70% cocoa solids)

½ x 135g pack orange-flavoured jelly

3 tbsp orange juice

zest of 1 orange, to decorate

1. Heat the oven to 180C/350F/gas 4. Line a muffin tin with six paper cases. Put the flour, sugar, egg, oil, yoghurt and orange zest into a mixing bowl and beat until smooth. Spoon the mixture into the cake case.

2. Bake for 15–20 minutes, or until risen, springy to the touch and a skewer inserted into the centre comes out clean. Leave to cool in the tin for a few minutes, then transfer to a wire rack to cool completely.

3. To make the orange topping, set a large heatproof bowl over a pan of barely simmering water and add the chocolate, jelly and orange juice and stir until the chocolate has melted and the topping is smooth. Spoon the topping over the cakes. Sprinkle with orange zest while the topping is still wet, then allow to set before eating.

MIDNIGHT'S CUPCAKES

CARDAMOM AND ROSE CUPCAKES

Y ou don't need to be a telepath to realise that these cardamom cupcakes are going to go down a treat. Even those without a superior sense of smell will appreciate the softly scented rose icing topped with crushed rose petals. Perfect for celebrating birthdays – or India's independence from colonial rule – their superpower is their exquisite taste sensation. Serve on the stroke of midnight.

Makes 12 cupcakes

250g/9oz soft butter
250g/9oz caster sugar
3 eggs, lightly beaten
250g/9oz self-raising flour
5 cardamom pods, seeds only
and bashed to a powder
zest and juice of 1 lemon

For the icing
200g/7oz icing sugar
2 tsp rosewater
pink food colouring
(optional)
crushed crystallised
rose petals

1. Heat the oven to 180C/350F/gas 4. Line a 12-hole cake tin with muffin cases. Put the cupcake ingredients into a bowl and beat with an electric whisk until smooth. Divide the cake mixture between the muffin cases and bake for 20 minutes, or until golden, risen and a skewer inserted into the centre comes out clean. Allow to cool for a few minutes then transfer to a wire rack to cool completely.

2. To make the icing, sift the icing sugar into a bowl and whisk in the rosewater and a little dab of pink food colouring. The icing should be thick but spreadable – if you need to add a little more liquid, add a tiny drop of rosewater or water. Spread the icing over the cooled cupcakes, then sprinkle over some crushed rose petals and allow the icing to set before serving.

THE WAR OF THE WALNUT WHIRLS

WALNUT WHIRLS

No one would have believed in the last years of the nineteenth century that in the future we would be creating these extra-terrestrial ordinary walnut whirls. They taste – quite simply – out of this world. Blast them with a heat ray before adding the Martian-mallows. I guarantee you'll always find space for them – even if that's a concept quite alien to you.

Makes 6–8 whirls

4 eggs
140g/5oz caster sugar
100g/4oz self-raising flour
2 tbsp cocoa powder
140g/5oz mini marshmallows
16 roasted walnut halves, plus
1 tbsp chopped walnuts
100g/4oz plain chocolate,
melted and cooled

1. Heat the oven to 190C/375F/gas 5. Grease and line a 25 x 35cm (10 x 14in) baking tray with baking paper. Whisk the eggs and sugar until pale and fluffy – about 5 minutes. Sift in the flour and cocoa powder and fold into the egg mixture.

2. Spread the mixture in the tin, smoothing the surface, then bake for 10–12 minutes or until springy to the touch. Cool for a few minutes in the tin, then transfer to a wire rack.

3. Use a 6–7cm (2.5in) round cutter to stamp out six circles from the cooled sponge. Set aside. Put the mini marshmallows and 2 tablespoons of water into a small bowl set over a pan of barely simmering water, and stir continuously with a wooden spoon until the marshmallows melt and become thick and shiny.

4. Put a teaspoonful of melted marshmallow onto each sponge base. Top with a couple of roasted walnut halves then evenly pile with melted marshmallow – use a fork to create dramatic swirls and a peak in the marshmallow. Put aside to cool and set – do not put in the fridge or the marshmallow will go soggy.

5. Spoon melted chocolate over the top of each walnut whirl and sprinkle over the extra chopped walnuts. Let the chocolate set before serving.

LIFE OF PECAN PIE

PECAN PIE WITH CHOCOLATE ICING

~~~~~~~~

This pecan pie is grrrrrreat! The base of pastry serves as a ship of dreams, into which a stormy sea of syrup mix is poured. The lightly toasted pecans and mixed spice, meanwhile, add an exotic twist – much like creatures in a zoo might do. (Richard) Parker yourself in a comfy armchair and enjoy a slice of this orange-brown-and-white, tiger-striped Pi. You'll be (ship)wrecked before you know it.

Serves 6–8

1 x 375g block ready-made sweet shortcrust pastry

flour, for dusting

175g/6oz soft light brown sugar

140g/5oz golden syrup

100g/4oz butter

½ tsp vanilla extract

½ tsp mixed spice

200g/7oz pecan nuts

3 eggs, lightly beaten

To finish

25g/1oz plain chocolate, roughly chopped

25g/1oz white chocolate, roughly chopped

1. Roll the pastry on a lightly floured work surface to 5mm thick and use to line a deep 23cm (9in) loose-bottomed tart tin. Trim the pastry and chill for 15 minutes, or until firm.

2. Put the sugar, syrup, butter, vanilla and mixed spice into a pan and heat gently until the butter has melted and the sugar has dissolved. Stir to combine. Remove from the heat and allow to cool slightly.

3. Heat the oven to 180C/350F/gas 4. Tip the pecans onto a baking tray and cook for 8 minutes, stirring halfway through the cooking time, or until lightly toasted. Remove from the oven and finely chop two-thirds of them, leaving the rest whole.

4. Beat the eggs into the syrup mixture then stir in the chopped pecans. Sit the pastry case on a baking sheet and pour the syrupy pecans into the shell. Arrange the whole pecans over the top then bake for 45–50 minutes, or until golden and set but with a slight wobble in the centre. Leave to cool to room temperature in the tin.

5. Put the plain chocolate and white chocolate into two separate microwave dishes and heat in 10-second bursts until melted. Use a teaspoon or small piping bag to pipe from the centre outwards to look like a tiger's stripes against the golden orange of the pecan pie filling. Allow to set before serving.

TWENTY THOUSAND LEAGUES UNDER THE SEED CAKE

LEMON AND POPPY SEED CAKE

~~~~~

T his is a sea monster of a seed cake, laced with lovely lemon and peppered with poppy seeds. Set sail on a great adventure – you'll find happiness rather than Nemo as you pick up your fork to take a bite. So pop up your periscope and dive in. I (sub)marine it.

Serves 6–8

200g/7oz soft butter
200g/7oz caster sugar
3 eggs, lightly beaten
zest and juice of 2 lemons
225g/8oz self-raising flour
2 tbsp poppy seeds

For the filling
200g/7oz cream cheese
50g/2oz soft butter
2 tbsp icing sugar
6 tbsp lemon curd
poppy seeds, to sprinkle

1. Heat the oven to 190C/375F/gas 5. Grease and line two 20cm (8in) round cake tins with baking paper. Cream the butter and sugar until pale and fluffy, then gradually add the eggs followed by the lemon zest and juice. Stir after each addition – your mixture might look like it has split, don't worry it will all come together. Add the flour and poppy seeds and stir to combine.

2. Divide the mixture between the tins, smooth the surface and bake for 20–25 minutes or until golden, risen and a skewer inserted into the centre comes out clean. Leave to cool in the tin for a few minutes, then transfer to a wire rack to cool completely.

3. To make the filling, beat the cream cheese, butter and icing sugar until soft, swirl through the lemon curd, then spread half of the mixture over one of the cakes, sandwich with the other cake and spread the remaining cream cheese icing over the top. Sprinkle with poppy seeds and serve.

'Soon her eye fell on a little glass box that was
lying under the table: she opened it, and found in
it a very small cake, on which the words "EAT ME"
were beautifully marked in currants.'

—

Lewis Carroll,
Alice's Adventures in Wonderland

CHILDREN'S CLASSICS

FLAPJACK & THE BEANSTALK

STICKY ORANGE FLAPJACKS

Once upon a time, some orange zest, butter, sugar and syrup were cooked up in a pan. Some magic beans in the shape of sunflower seeds were thrown onto a field of oats and – lo! – in the morning there grew a giant bake. When Jack cut into it, he enjoyed the golden-syrup taste so much that he went back for more – and more. Now every time he bakes, you can hear him cry, 'Fee, fi, fo, fum, I smell the scent of a flapjack – yum!' And they all lived happily ever after.

Makes 18 flapjacks

250g/9oz butter, plus extra for greasing
zest of 2 oranges
250g/9oz caster sugar
175g/6oz golden syrup
425g/15oz porridge oats
2 tbsp sunflower seeds
3 tbsp fine-shred marmalade

1. Grease and line a 20 x 30cm (8 x 12in) baking tin with baking paper. Heat the oven to 180C/350F/gas 4. Put the orange zest, butter, sugar and syrup into a pan and heat until the butter has melted and all of the ingredients are fully combined. Remove from the heat and stir in the oats to coat in the syrup.

2. Tip the oaty mixture into the tin, sprinkle over the sunflower seeds then bake for 25 minutes, or until the flapjack has turned a deep golden colour at the edges. Leave to cool completely in the tin.

3. Loosen the marmalade with a tablespoon of boiling water, mix until smooth then brush over the flapjack. Put the flapjack on a board and cut into squares before serving.

CHARLIE & THE CHOCOLATE BROWNIE

HAZELNUT BLONDIES

~~~~~~

Y ou'll need a Bucket-load of these hazelnut and white chocolate brownies to keep up with demand! A bake as good as anything Willy Wonka might have invented in his famous factory, these are so easy to make that you won't need your own army of Oompa-Loompas to rustle them up. So grab yourself a Golden Ticket and get munching. Just remember the cautionary tale of Augustus Gloop – and I'm not (Grandpa) Joe-king.

Makes 20 blondies

400g/14oz white chocolate
75g/2½oz butter
3 eggs, lightly beaten
175g/6oz caster sugar
175g/6oz self-raising flour
175g/6oz blanched hazelnuts, roughly chopped
1 tsp vanilla extract
chocolate ice cream, to serve

1. Heat the oven to 190C/375F/gas 5. Grease and line a 20 x 30cm (8 x 12in) baking tin with baking paper.

2. Roughly chop half of the chocolate and set aside. Place the remaining chocolate and butter in a heatproof bowl set over a pan of barely simmering water and stir to melt and combine. Remove from the heat and allow to cool for a few minutes.

3. Whisk together the eggs and sugar in a large bowl until pale and creamy, then gradually beat in the melted chocolate mixture. Gently fold in the flour and a pinch of salt until no flour remains visible. Add the chopped chocolate, hazelnuts and vanilla extract and stir to combine.

4. Scrape the mixture into the baking tin, smooth the surface and bake for 25–30 minutes until risen and golden and the centre is firm to the touch, but still lightly fudgy underneath.

5. Leave to cool in the tin for about 30 minutes, then remove and cut into squares. Serve warm with a scoop of bitter chocolate ice cream – if you dare.

THE HOBBISCUIT

PISTACHIO BISCUITS

A ll great quests end with a feast fit for a hobbit, and with these pistachio biscuits the search for tasty treasure is over. They're hot stuff – even without the fire-breathing dragon. They're also great for gifts, so why not wrap them up and tie a (Bil)bo around them? Or you can simply use them to fill the hobbit hole in your own stomach.

If the biscuit tin's your destination, head There and Back Again for a taste sensation that's Shire joy from first bite to last.

Makes 12 biscuits

25g pistachios, plus 1 tbsp, chopped
50g/2oz caster sugar
100g/4oz butter, softened
140g/5oz self-raising flour

1. Put the pistachios into the bowl of a food processor with half the sugar and whizz until finely ground. Tip out into a bowl and add the remaining caster sugar and the butter. Beat until pale and fluffy then stir in the flour.

2. Line a couple of baking trays with baking paper. Roll tablespoons of biscuit dough into ball and place them on the baking trays, leaving space between them for spreading. Flatten the balls slightly with your fingers, push in a few chopped pistachios and chill for 15 minutes.

3. Heat the oven to 200C/400F/gas 5 and when hot, bake the biscuits for 10 minutes. Remove from the oven and allow to firm up on the trays for a few minutes before transferring them to a wire rack to cool and crisp.

WATERSHIP UPSIDE-DOWN CAKE

SPICED PLUM UPSIDE-DOWN CAKE

~~~

Y ou don't need 'Bright Eyes' – or the extra-sensory perception of young Fiver – to realise this spiced plum upside-down cake is as lush as new-mown grass, so I won't rabbit on about it. The search for the perfect home-sweet-home sweet ends here.

Now buck up your ideas and doe the only thing you can, which is of course to hop to it and tuck in. But just be warned – it's so enticing it may ensnare you …

Serves 6–8

75g/2½oz butter
75g/2½oz soft light brown sugar
½ tsp ground cinnamon
6 firm ripe plums, halved, stones discarded

For the sponge
100g/4oz soft butter
100g/4oz soft light brown sugar
2 eggs, lightly beaten
100g/4oz self-raising flour
½ tsp ground cinnamon
1 tsp vanilla extract
pouring cream, to serve

1. Preheat the oven to 180C/350F/gas 4. Grease a 20cm round cake tin. Put the butter, sugar and cinnamon in a non-stick frying pan over a medium heat and stir until the sugar has dissolved. Add the plums, cut side down and cook for 2–3 minutes, or until just starting to soften. Remove from the heat and pour the plums and any caramel into the cake tin, flip the plums so that they are all cut side down. Set aside.

2. To make the cake put all of the sponge ingredients into a bowl and beat until smooth. Spoon on top of the plums and smooth the surface. Bake for 30–35 minutes, or until risen and a skewer inserted into the centre comes out clean. Remove from the oven and cool for 5 minutes, place a large serving plate on top of the cake and flip the whole thing upside down to turn out. You may have to reposition some of the plums, and scrape any of the remaining syrup from the tin. Serve warm with pouring cream.

THE RED VELVETEEN RABBIT

RED VELVET LAYER CAKE

~~~~~

There is nothing more beloved than the scarlet layers of this spectacular bake. It's a Real childhood favourite, and so feverishly tasty you'll want to bless its little cottontails. Burrow into this colourful cake with emphatic enthusiasm – don't toy with it – and enjoy *lapin* it up.

Serves 12–14

375g/13oz plain flour
50g/2oz cocoa powder
3 tsp baking powder
½ tsp bicarbonate of soda
175g/6oz butter
300g/11oz caster sugar
2 tsp vanilla extract
1–2 tsp red food colouring paste
3 eggs, lightly beaten
300ml/½ pint buttermilk
1 tsp cider vinegar

1. Heat the oven to 180C/350F/gas 4. Grease and line the base of four 20cm (8in) round cake tins with baking paper.

2. Put the flour, cocoa, baking powder and bicarbonate of soda in a big bowl and use a whisk to combine. Set aside. In another bowl, beat the butter and sugar until pale and creamy, then add the vanilla extract and enough food colouring to give a deep red colour. Gradually add the eggs, alternating with tablespoons of the flour and cocoa mixture. Fold in the rest of the flour mix, then stir in the buttermilk and vinegar.

3. Divide the mixture between the tins and smooth the surfaces. Bake for 30 minutes or until well risen, firm to the touch and a skewer inserted into the middle comes out clean. Remove from the oven, allow to cool in the tins for a few minutes then transfer to wire racks to cool completely.

For the cream cheese icing

200g/7oz full-fat cream cheese

250g/9oz unsalted butter, softened

600g/1lb 5oz icing sugar, sifted

2 tsp vanilla extract

red sprinkles, to decorate

4. To make the icing, beat the cream cheese and butter until very soft and light, then gradually add in the icing sugar. This may feel quite stiff to start with, but keep beating and it will eventually soften and become extremely light and fluffy. Add the vanilla extract and beat for at least 5 minutes – this will ensure the icing is of sufficient volume to fill and cover the cake.

5. To assemble the cake, sandwich together all the layers with some of the icing, then use the remainder to cover the top and sides. Decorate lavishly with red sprinkles.

APPLES' ADVENTURES IN CRUMBLE-LAND

CINNAMON AND APPLE CRUMB CAKE

~~~~~~~

Take a tumble down a rabbit hole into the magical world of the Mad Hatter's Tea Party. What better scrumptiousness to find at the end of it than a piping-hot cinnamon-scented apple crumb cake? Line up the fruity emerald orbs and prepare the shining blade … Now off with their heads!

It's certainly a dish fit for a Red Queen, and demands just one thing: Eat Me.

Serves 8

140g/5oz soft butter, plus extra for greasing
250g/9oz self-raising flour
1 tsp ground cinnamon
¼ tsp ground cloves
¼ tsp ground nutmeg
140g/5oz soft light brown sugar
2 eggs
100ml/3½fl oz milk
2 eating apples, peeled, cored and sliced

1. Heat the oven to 180C/350F/gas 4. Grease and line the base of a deep, loose-bottomed 20cm (8in) round cake tin with baking paper. Combine the flour and spices and set aside. In another bowl, beat the butter and sugar until light and fluffy, then gradually add the eggs, alternating with a tablespoon of the flour and spice mixture. Fold in the rest of the flour and spices then pour in the milk and stir until smooth.

2. Tip the batter into the tin, arrange the apple slices on top and bake for 20 minutes.

3. Meanwhile, make the crumble topping. Rub the butter into the flour, spices and sugar so that some small lumps of butter remain, then stir in the pecans and set aside. After 20 minutes, remove the cake from the oven and sprinkle the crumble over

For the crumble topping
25g/1oz unsalted butter
75g/2½oz self-raising flour
½ tsp ground cinnamon
pinch of ground cloves
pinch of ground nutmeg
75g/2½oz Demerara sugar
50g/2oz pecan nuts, finely chopped
crème fraîche, to serve

the apple slices. Return to the oven and cook for 40 minutes or until the cake is firm to the touch and a skewer inserted into the middle comes out clean. Leave to cool in the tin for 30 minutes, then remove and place on a serving plate. Serve warm with crème fraîche.

JAMES & THE GIANT PEACH COBBLER

PEACH, RASPBERRY AND MANDARIN COBBLER

T his is no place for a basic Sponge (or Spiker). Take yourself on a magical journey with this imaginative peach cobbler, bursting with character and flavour and even surprising elements ... like raspberries and mandarins. This is a dish as luxurious as Silk(worm) and as appetising as the Big Apple. It'll put you on cloud nine – but just watch out for those spoilsport Cloud Men as you savour your snack!

Serves 6–8

2 x 400g cans peach halves in juice, drained and juice reserved and thickly sliced

1 x 200g can mandarin segments in juice, drained

1 tsp ground cinnamon

1 tbsp cornflour

100g/4oz frozen raspberries, defrosted

½ tsp almond extract

For the cobbler

50g/2oz butter, diced

175g/6oz self-raising flour

25g/1oz ground almonds

50g/2oz caster sugar, plus extra to dust

85ml/3fl oz milk, plus extra to glaze

25g/1oz flaked almonds

vanilla ice cream, to serve (optional)

1. Heat the oven to 190C/375F/gas 5. Put the peach slices, mandarin segments and cinnamon into a rectangular oven dish. Add 100ml (3½fl oz) of juice from the peaches, sprinkle over the cornflour and stir. Bake for 10 minutes.

2. Meanwhile, make the cobbler. Rub the butter into the flour until it resembles fine breadcrumbs. Stir in the ground almonds and sugar then add enough milk to form a soft dough. Tip out onto a floured surface, knead briefly then cut into 12 equal parts. Roll each one into rough ball shapes.

3. Stir the raspberries into the peach and mandarin mix. Place the cobbles over the the fruit, brush with a little milk, sprinkle with caster sugar and flaked almonds. Bake for 20 minutes, or until the cobbles are golden and the fruit is bubbling. Serve with vanilla ice cream, if you like.

PETER PANETTONE

CHOCOLATE AND ORANGE PANETTONE

~~~~~~

Darlings, this panettone will give you a childlike delight in pudding all over again – almost as if you never grew up. There's no need to Tinker(bell) with the recipe; this has been a classic bake since 1919. You'll fall for it Hook, line and sinker. So pick up the second spoon to the right and eat straight on till morning.

Serves 8–10

100ml/3½fl oz milk

200g/7oz butter, softened, plus extra for greasing

100g/4oz caster sugar

zest of 2 large oranges

2 tsp vanilla extract

5 eggs, lightly beaten

500g/1lb 2oz strong white bread flour, plus extra for dusting

2 x 7g sachets fast-action yeast

200g/7oz plain chocolate, roughly chopped

100g/4oz mixed peel, finely chopped

1 egg white

icing sugar, to dust

1. Heat the milk to just below boiling point then remove from the heat. Beat the butter, sugar, orange zest and vanilla extract until pale and creamy. Gradually beat in the eggs and heated milk, then set aside.

2. In a large bowl, combine the flour, sugar and yeast with a good pinch of salt. Make a well in the centre of the flour and gradually pour in the wet ingredients, stirring to form a soft sticky dough. Knead briefly to bring the dough together then cover with a clean cloth and leave to stand in a warm spot until doubled in size.

3. Grease and line the base of a 20–23cm (8–9in) springform deep cake tin with baking paper. Wrap the outside of the cake tin with a double layer of baking paper that extends about 10cm (4in) above the top of the tin. Secure with string and set aside.

4. Tip out the dough onto a floured work surface and knead briefly to get rid of any air bubbles. Add the chopped chocolate and mixed peel, kneading, folding and pushing the chocolate and peel into the dough as you go. Shape the dough into a round and drop into the prepared cake tin. Cover loosely with a cloth and leave to stand for about an hour or until doubled in size.

5. Heat the oven to 180C/350F/gas 4. Brush the top of the panettone with the egg white. Bake for 1 hour–1¼ hours or until risen, dark golden brown and a skewer inserted in the centre comes out clean. (Cover with foil after 45 minutes if your panettone is getting too dark). Remove from the oven and allow to cool for 15 minutes in the tin, then transfer to a wire rack to cool completely. Dust with icing sugar before serving in slices.

HARRY POTTER & THE PHILOSOPHER'S STREUSEL

CINNAMON CRANBERRY STREUSEL

～～～

No need to Muggle your way through this recipe, because it's super simple. This Streusel-That-Must-Not-Be-Named will cast a spell on all who enjoy it – and I'm not having you Ron… Whip up a magical Potion of cinnamon and cranberry to Transfigure a dish that's wonderfully wizard. It'll open a (Dumble)dore into a world of streusels you never knew existed. Now *that's* magic.

Serves 12

350g/12oz butter, softened, plus extra for greasing
75g/2½oz caster sugar
3 tbsp olive oil
1 tsp vanilla extract
1 egg, lightly beaten
700g/1lb 9oz plain flour, plus extra for dusting
1½ tsp baking powder
½ tsp salt
1 tbsp ground cinnamon

1. First make the cranberry sauce. Place the cranberries in a food processor with the sugar and whizz until roughly chopped. Tip into a pan with the orange juice and mixed spice. Bring to the boil, stirring constantly, then reduce the heat and cook for a further 5 minutes. Remove from the heat and allow to cool.

2. To make the streusel dough, cream the butter and sugar together in a bowl until pale and fluffy, then pour in the olive oil and vanilla extract and gradually beat in the egg. Combine the flour, baking powder, salt and cinnamon in a bowl then gradually stir this into the wet ingredients to form a dough. Knead briefly in the bowl to bring the dough together, then wrap in cling film and chill for at least 2 hours or until firm.

For the cranberry sauce
225g/8oz fresh or frozen cranberries
75g/2½oz caster sugar
juice of I orange
½ tsp ground mixed spice
icing sugar, to dust

3. Heat the oven to 150C/300F/gas 2. Grease and line the base of a 25cm (10in) round springform cake tin with baking paper. Grease and flour the sides of the tin. Divide the chilled dough in half, put one half back in the fridge then coarsely grate the other half into the tin to cover the bottom in an even layer.

4. Carefully spoon the cranberry sauce over the grated dough, leaving Icm (½in) clear all around the edge of the tin. Grate the remaining streusel dough evenly over the top. Bake for 1¼–1½ hours until pale but firm. Dust the streusel with icing sugar whilst still hot. Leave to cool in the tin, then remove and cut into wedges to serve.

*'Do you think because you are virtuous,
that there shall be no more cakes and ale?'*
—

William Shakespeare, *Twelfth Night*

PLAYS

MUCH ADO ABOUT MUFFINS

DOUBLE CHOCOLATE MUFFINS

I do love nothing in the world so well as muffins – and what could be more fitting for this double-wedding comedy than a double-chocolate treat? (There's a double meaning in that.) Perhaps you could even go for a Shakespearean twist and make them civil as a chocolate orange …

While they're guaranteed to make you a Hero in the kitchen, just be warned that your guests could soon start sparring for the last one – with pastry forks as sharp as the wicked wit of Benedict and Beatrice.

Makes 12 muffins

300g/11oz dark chocolate (at least 70% cocoa solids), roughly chopped
375g/13oz self-raising flour
50g/2oz cocoa powder
75g/2½oz soft light brown sugar
300ml/½ pint milk
6 tbsp vegetable oil
2 eggs, lightly beaten
1 tsp vanilla extract
100g/4oz white chocolate, roughly chopped

1. Heat the oven to 190C/375F/gas 5. Line a 12-hole muffin tray with paper cases. Put half the dark chocolate in a heatproof bowl set over a pan of barely simmering water and stir until smooth and melted. Remove from the heat and allow to cool. In another bowl mix the flour, cocoa and sugar.

2. Make a well in the centre of the dry ingredients then add the milk, oil, eggs and vanilla extract. Stir to combine then fold in the cooled melted chocolate. Tip in the chopped dark and white chocolates and stir until combined.

3. Divide the mixture among the paper cases and bake for 25 minutes or until the muffins are risen and a skewer inserted into the centre comes out clean. Transfer to a wire rack to cool and serve warm or at room temperature.

THE TAMING OF THE CHOUX

CHURROS

~~~

Y ou could find yourself in hot oil if you choose to marry a bit of a doughnut, but these choux-based churros have a happy-ever-after ending. Tamed by the piping bag of Petruchio, there's nothing but sunny tempers and melt-in-the-mouth goodness on display here. They're so delicious you may find yourself eagerly declaring the Sun to be the Moon, a man to be a woman, and a feminist reading to be overly uptight, simply to secure another blissful mouthful of these play-ful treats.

Makes 24 churros

85g/3oz butter, diced
140g/5oz plain flour, sifted
3 eggs, lightly beaten

To finish
1 litre /1¾ pints sunflower oil
100g/4oz caster sugar

1. Put the butter into a medium-sized pan with 225ml (8fl oz) water and heat gently to melt the butter. Once melted, increase the heat and bring to the boil. Remove from the heat, add the flour and beat the mixture until you get a smooth, shiny dough that leaves the sides of the pan. Tip into a mixing bowl and allow to cool for 5 minutes.

2. Gradually add the eggs and continue to beat until you have a smooth dough that falls reluctantly from the spoon. Pile into a piping bag fitted with a 1cm (½in) star-shaped nozzle and set aside to rest for 15 minutes.

3. Pour the oil into a deep medium-sized pan to a depth of about 5cm (2in) and heat to 180C/350F. Quickly dip the end of a pair of kitchen scissors into the hot oil, then hold the piping bag with one hand about 5cm (2in) above the surface of the oil. Squeeze out the dough and use the heated scissors to cut strips at 10cm (4in) intervals. Do this in batches, frying them for 2–3 minutes or until golden and puffed up. Remove with a slotted spoon and drain on kitchen paper. Roll the warm shrew's tails in the caster sugar and serve.

THE CRU-SYLLABUB

LEMON AND STRAWBERRY SYLLABUB

D ark forces have clearly been at work here, whipping up a gossipy storm of the lightest lemon and most succulent strawberries. Be a Goody Two-Shoes no longer, but give in to your inner wicked witch. This syllabub is so devilishly tasty it's worth it. You'll willingly put your name to it, come hell or high water, hurricane or (Abi)gail. So Miller over it no more; don't make it a trial. Poppet into your mouth. You have your lemony goodness now.

Serves 6

400ml/14fl oz double cream
200g tub Greek yoghurt
75g/3½oz caster sugar
1 tsp vanilla extract
75ml/2½fl oz sweet wine (such as vin santo), plus a drizzle
juice and zest of 1 lemon
grapes, halved, to serve
strawberries, hulled and chopped, to serve
handful toasted flaked almonds, to sprinkle

1. Whip the cream, yoghurt, caster sugar and vanilla extract to soft peaks. Fold in the wine with the lemon juice and zest until fully combined.

2. Put the fruit into the base of six serving glasses and drizzle with a little wine. Spoon the syllabub over the top and sprinkle with toasted almonds to serve. Perfect with biscotti and sweet wine.

CAT ON A TARTE TATIN ROOF

CARAMELISED APPLE TARTE TATIN

O n a hot summer's evening in the Mississippi Delta, nothing tastes as fine as this caramelised tarte tatin. The accompanying ice cream may melt faster than the family ties in the Pollitt clan, but it's still a Big Daddy of a dish that'll have you feline good in no time. So cut yourself a Brick of a slice as you divide up the estate, plant(ation) yourself at the table with a spoon, and dig in.

Serves 6

225g/8oz ready-rolled puff pastry

For the filling
75g/2½oz caster sugar
4–5 small eating apples, peeled and cored
50g/2oz butter, diced
vanilla ice cream, to serve

1. To make the filling, put the sugar and 3 tablespoons of water in a pan set over a low heat and let it dissolve, stirring occasionally, then increase the heat and, without stirring, cook the syrup to a rich golden caramel. Carefully pour it into a shallow, heavy-based, 20cm (8in) round cake tin or an ovenproof frying pan and swirl the caramel to coat the base evenly.

2. Heat the oven to 220C/425F/gas 7. Dot the caramel with half of the butter. Arrange the apple halves curved side down on top, packing them tightly. Fill any gaps with smaller apple wedges. Dot over the remaining butter. Place the tin or frying pan over a medium heat and cook for 5 minutes to par-cook and lightly brown the apples. Make sure the apples do not burn.

3. Lay the pastry over the apples, then trim it around the edge of the pan or tin and tuck it inside the rim. Bake for 20–25 minutes until the pastry is well risen, crisp and golden brown.

4. Allow to cool for 10 minutes, then invert a serving plate over the pan and carefully flip the whole thing over, lifting the pan to reveal caramelised apples. Spoon over any caramel sauce left in the pan, cut the tarte tatin into wedges and serve warm with vanilla ice cream.

ROULADE & JULIET

ALMOND, APRICOT AND ROSE ROULADE

'A rose by any other name would smell as sweet ...' and this rose-flavoured roulade tastes as sweet as teenage crush, as lovers' kiss, as moonlit balcony embrace. If you've the Will, there's a way to impress your guests, and this star-crossed sweet of almonds and apricots is it.

So Nurse your slice with all the fanaticism of a friar at a secret wedding. Till death-by-chocolate-chips do us part ...

Serves 8

25g/1oz flaked almonds
4 eggs, separated
175g/6oz caster sugar, plus extra for dusting
1 tsp vanilla extract
100g/4oz marzipan, grated
3 tbsp plain flour

For the filling
2 tbsp Amaretto
1 tsp rosewater
300g/11oz crème fraîche
6 ripe apricots, halved, stoned and chopped
1 tsp rosewater
chocolate chips, to decorate
crystallised rose petals, to decorate

1. Heat the oven to 180C/350F/gas 4. Grease and line a 33 x 23cm (13 x 9in) Swiss roll tin with non-stick baking paper, scatter with flaked almonds and set aside.

2. Whisk the egg yolks with 125g (5oz) of the sugar until pale and fluffy. Stir in the vanilla and marzipan, then fold in the flour.

3. In a clean bowl, whisk the egg whites to stiff peaks then gradually add the remaining sugar, whisking after each addition.

4. Using a large metal spoon, carefully fold a quarter of the egg whites into the almond mixture to loosen, then fold in the rest. Tip the mixture into the tin and lightly spread in an even layer. Bake for 20 minutes or until well risen and just firm to the touch. Remove from the oven and cool for a few minutes.

5. Lay another piece of baking paper on a flat surface, dust with caster sugar then tip out the roulade onto it. Peel away the original paper and leave the roulade to cool.

6. Drizzle the Amaretto and rosewater over the roulade, then spread it with crème fraîche and dot over the apricots. Starting with one of the short ends, roll up the roulade, using the paper to help you. Roll the roulade onto a serving plate, seam side down. Dust the top with more caster sugar and sprinkle over the chocolate chips and some rose petals for a final flourish.

MIDSUMMER PUDDING'S DREAM

SUMMER PUDDING

~~~~~~

Take two lovely berries moulded on a stem, multiply, and use liberally in this fairy-fabulous Midsummer pudding. Before, the bread was milk-white, now purple with love's wound and the colourful, vibrant juices of succulent redcurrants, blackcurrants and raspberries. While the course of true love never did run smooth, the mechanicals of this dish should be so straightforward that even an ass could make it. Give me your hands and charge your glasses to toast its tastiness. All cry as one: 'Bottoms up!'

Serves 6–8

450g/1lb raspberries
225g/8oz redcurrants
225g/8oz blackcurrants
75g/2½oz caster sugar
8 stale slices white bread from a large loaf, crusts removed
extra berries and double cream, to serve

1. Put the raspberries in a saucepan with the redcurrants, blackcurrants, sugar and 3 tablespoons of water. Cook over a medium heat for 3–4 minutes or until the juices begin to run. Remove from the heat and set aside.

2. Cut a round from one of the slices of bread to fit the base of a 1.5 litre (2¾ pint) pudding basin. Cut the remaining slices in half lengthways. Arrange almost all the bread slices around the side of the pudding basin – leaving enough for the top – overlapping them slightly at the bottom, so they fit together neatly and tightly. Position the round of bread to cover the hole in the base.

3. Strain the fruit and spoon about 100ml (3½fl oz) of the fruit juice into a jug. Set aside. Spoon the remaining fruit and juice into the bread-lined pudding basin. Cover completely with the remaining bread slices, trimming them to fit as necessary. Cover with cling film, then sit a plate on top of the pudding and weigh it down with a couple of cans of beans. Leave to stand in the fridge overnight.

4. To serve the pudding, first remove the weights, plate and cling film. Invert a serving plate over the pudding basin, hold the two firmly together and flip over. Give them a firm shake (up and down, rather than side to side), then lift off the pudding basin. Cut into wedges and serve with a few extra berries and some double cream.

MAD HATTER'S TEA PARTY

Embrace the madness with these wonderful
bakes. Every one a little out of the ordinary …

~~~~~

TO KILL A BATTENBERG

Chocolate and almond Battenberg cake (see page 68)

—

THE COLOR PROFITEROLES

Purple profiteroles with white chocolate icing (see page 78)

—

MIDDLEMARSHMALLOWS

Peppermint marshmallows (see page 75)

~~~~~

Serve with Pink Punch …
To whip up a jug of pink punch, throw 200g/7oz
raspberries into a blender with the juice and zest
of 1 lemon, 50ml/2fl oz crème de framboise,
100ml/4fl oz vodka and mix with 1 litre/
1¾ pints natural lemonade and lots of ice.

THE BIRTHDAY PARTY CAKE

CARROT CAKE

~~~~~~

This …

      is …

            a …

                delicious …

                      cake.

Serves 6–8

225g/8oz soft butter
225g/8oz caster sugar
4 eggs, lightly beaten
zest of 1 orange,
plus 1 tbsp juice
175g/6oz self-raising flour
1 tsp baking powder
½ tsp ground allspice
½ tsp ground cinnamon
50g/2oz ground almonds
350g/12oz carrots, grated
100g/4oz Brazil nuts, roughly
chopped

For the topping
250g/9oz mascarpone cheese
zest of 1 orange and
2 tbsp juice
2 tbsp icing sugar

1. Heat the oven to 180C/350F/gas 4. Grease and line the base of two 18cm (7in) round cake tins with baking paper. Beat the butter and sugar together until pale and fluffy. Gradually add the eggs, orange zest and juice and stir to combine. Add the flour, baking powder, spices and ground almonds to the wet ingredients and mix well. Stir in the carrots and chopped nuts.

2. Divide the mixture between the prepared cake tins, smooth the surface then bake for 35–40 minutes or until risen and a skewer inserted into the centre comes out clean. Allow to cool in the tin for a few minutes then transfer to a wire rack to cool completely.

3. To make the topping, beat the mascarpone, orange zest and juice with the icing sugar until smooth. Use half to sandwich the cakes together, then spread the remaining icing over the top. Chill until ready to serve.

WAITING FOR GÂTEAU

HAZELNUT MERINGUE GÂTEAU

You'll be Lucky to get a slice of this enigmatic Hazelnut Meringue Gâteau. The recipe indicates it takes an hour to bake, but you may have to wait for it – just like Vladimir and Estragon. Once the instructions have been followed, there's nothing to be done. But something will turn up in the end. Let's hope it is a cake.

Serves 8–10

5 egg whites
250g/9oz caster sugar
½ tsp mixed spice
140g/5oz blanched toasted hazelnuts, roughly chopped
75g/2½oz plain chocolate, roughly chopped
75g/2½oz white chocolate, roughly chopped

To finish
300ml/½ pint double cream
200g/7oz raspberries
handful blanched toasted hazelnuts, roughly chopped

1. Heat the oven to 140C/275F/gas 1. Line a couple of baking sheets with non-stick baking paper. Draw a 23cm (9in) circle on one piece of paper and a 17cm (7in) circle on the other. Turn the pieces of paper over.

2. To make the meringue, whisk the egg whites until stiff peaks. Gradually whisk in the sugar and spice, whisking between each addition to dissolve the sugar until you have very stiff, glossy meringues. Carefully fold in the chopped nuts and chocolate.

3. Spread the meringue over the marked circles. Swirl the edges of the large meringue and the whole surface of the small one with a palette knife. Bake for 1 hour or until puffed, lightly golden and firm. Open the oven door slightly and leave the meringues inside to cool completely.

4. To assemble the meringue gâteau, lightly whip the cream to soft peaks. Spread the largest meringue with two-thirds of the cream, scatter over a handful of raspberries, then sandwich with the other meringue. Spread the top of the smaller meringue with the remaining cream, dot with raspberries and scatter with hazelnuts.

THE CHERRY PIE ORCHARD

CHERRY PIE

～～～～

Chekhov your shopping list to ensure you've got all the ingredients below, then prepare this delectable pie which will appeal to the aristocracy and the bourgeoisie in equal measure. Pack it full of pitted cherries – the ripened fruit from a former way of life – and gather the cast of characters. Procrastinate until this treasured dish is sliced and diced and divided up like the cherry orchard itself.

Serves 8

500g block ready-made shortcrust pastry

1 tbsp cornflour

2 x 425g cans pitted cherries, drained and juice reserved

1 tsp vanilla extract

1 egg, lightly beaten, to glaze

25g/1oz Demerara sugar

pouring cream, to serve

1. Heat the oven to 190C/375F/gas 5. Roll out two-thirds of the pastry to a 5mm thickness and use to line a deep, 23cm (9in) pie dish. Trim off any excess pastry around the rim. Scrunch up a piece of baking paper and lay it on top of the pastry, then fill with baking beans and bake for 10 minutes. Remove from the oven, lift out the baking paper and beans and bake the pastry, uncovered, for a further 5 minutes until pale golden.

2. Meanwhile, mix the cornflour with a tablespoon of reserved cherry juice then add it to a pan with a further 100ml (3½fl oz) and the vanilla extract. Stir frequently and bring to the boil. Add the cherries and cook for a further minute until they are coated in the syrup. Leave to cool for a few minutes then pile the cherries and sauce into the pastry shell.

3. Roll out the remaining one-third of the pastry to a 5mm thickness, brush the edge of the pie with beaten egg, lay the pastry over the pie, trim, then press around the edge with a fork to secure. Cut a hole in the centre of the pie lid to allow steam to escape. Brush the top with egg and sprinkle with the Demerara sugar. Return to the oven and cook for a further 15–20 minutes or until golden and crisp. Serve with pouring cream.

INDEX

Virgin Books, an imprint of Ebury Publishing,
20 Vauxhall Bridge Road,
London SW1V 2SA

Virgin Books is part of the Penguin
Random House group of companies whose
addresses can be found at
global.penguinrandomhouse.com

Penguin
Random House
UK

Copyright © Ebury Publishing 2015

This book contains adapted recipes previously
published and owned by Ebury Publishing

First published in Great Britain by Virgin
Books in 2015

www.eburypublishing.co.uk

A CIP catalogue record for this book is
available from the British Library

ISBN 9780753556146

Printed and bound in Italy by
Printer Trento S.r.l.

MIX
Paper from
responsible sources
FSC
www.fsc.org   FSC® C018179

Penguin Random House is committed to a
sustainable future for our business, our readers
and our planet. This book is made from Forest
Stewardship Council® certified paper.

New recipes and adaptations of existing
recipes: Rosie Reynolds
Introductions and other text: Kate Moore
Design: Jilly Topping
Illustrations: Katt Frank